Cultivating
the Ch'i

CHANG SAN-FENG
Wu-T'ang Temple,
Hupei Province, China

Cultivating the Ch'i

Chen Kung Series

VOLUME ONE

Compiled and Translated by
Stuart Alve Olson
Revised, Expanded Edition

Dragon Door Publications
St. Paul

Published by
Dragon Door Publications
Box 4381
St. Paul, Minnesota 55104 U.S.A.
© 1993 by Stuart Alve Olson

Third edition (June 1993)
Library of Congress Catalog Card Number: 93-72185
ISBN 0-938045-11-3
First edition (1986)
Second edition (January 1992)
Cover Design by Lightbourne Images
Printed in the United States of America
Printed by Gopher State Litho, Minneapolis, MN
Printed on acid-free paper.

Acknowledgements

I would like to thank Master Tung-tsai Liang for all his initial help with translating many difficult terms and for his calligraphy used with the cover design and chapter headings. His kind help and encouragement will be forever appreciated.

Much appreciation is due to John Du Cane, without whom neither this book nor Dragon Door Publications would exist. He spent many hours organizing, proofing and editing the material. Indeed, he coiled about the obstacles of such projects like a dragon.

To Richard Peterson for his very exceptional photography. Truly a master of the lens. Because of his patience and generous efforts the exercises in this book have come to life. I am very grateful for his expert input.

Many thanks are due to Mike Urseth for his many hours of data entry and formatting, along with providing much required patience in dealing with all the misconceptions and changes.

Fred Marych for his cover painting and drawings. Most incredibly he managed to paint what my mind saw, transmitted only by a telephone conversation.

To Vern Petersen for his years of insisting that I again publish my books and for all his kind and generous help to that end. To Larry Hawkins who relentlessly encouraged both my writing and teaching. Deep appreciation to my wife, Lian Hwa, who has demonstrated great patience and understanding by allowing me to stay home and just work on books. Finally, many thanks to all my students, who through their support and diligent efforts, have been a source of inspiration for me. To all of them and to the others mentioned above, I bow in deep respect and gratitude.

— Translator

Yang Family Lineage

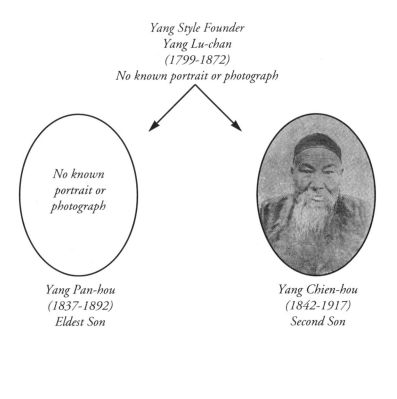

Yang Style Founder
Yang Lu-chan
(1799-1872)
No known portrait or photograph

No known
portrait or
photograph

Yang Pan-hou
(1837-1892)
Eldest Son

Yang Chien-hou
(1842-1917)
Second Son

Yang Shao-hou
(1862-1930)
Eldest Son of Yang Chien-hou

Yang Cheng-fu
(1883-1936)
Third Son of Yang Chien-hou

Translator's Lineage

Yang Shao-hou
(1862 -1930)

Yang Cheng-fu
(1883 - 1936)

Hsiung Yang-ho
(1886-1984)

Cheng Man-ch'ing
(1901-1975)

Liang Tung-tsai
(1900-)

Stuart Alve Olson
(1950 -)

By the Sea of Java dwells a living dragon,
*   Oh Khong Hwie,*
Your kung-fu, healing the poor.
Within "rusty iron" is pure steel.
Even the gods lower their heads
*   To a true man.*

Cultivating the Ch'i
The Secrets of Energy and Vitality

Translator's Introduction 11

Chapter One:..27
T'ai Chi Ch'uan and Nourishing Life
The Importance and Benefits of Practicing T'ai Chi Ch'uan
- T'ai Chi and other Chinese martial arts - The role of softness and gentleness - The health benefits of T'ai Chi - The Taoist concept of Nourishing Life - The principles of correct practice - Important T'ai Chi terms explained.

Chapter Two:..37
Discourse on Mind-Intent and Ch'i
The Relationship Between Mind, Mind-Intent and Ch'i
- The importance of ch'i - Ch'i and blood circulation - The difference between mind and mind-intent - Ch'i and mind-intent - The role of imagination - Some fundamental principles for cultivating ch'i - The tan-tien and ch'i - Different types of ch'i - Ch'i and the classics - Explanation of key Taoist terms.

Chapter Three: 47
Internal Breathing Methods for Mobilizing the Ch'i
Aspects of Breath and the Development of Ch'i
- Upper and lower level breathing - How to breathe correctly - How breath relates to ch'i - Breathing with the postures - Breathing with Pushing-Hands - Two ways to mobilize the ch'i - Issuing energy - Heng and Ha: the sounds of breath - How to use Heng and Ha - Commentary on Chinese breathing terminology.

Chapter Four: 57
T'ai Chi Ch'uan and Meditation
The Role of Seated Meditation in
Connection with T'ai Chi Ch'uan
The value of meditation - The similarities between T'ai
Chi and seated meditation - Internal and external
cultivation - Correct sitting practice - Four ways to
circulate ch'i - Explanation of Taoist meditation terms.

Chapter Five 75
T'ai Chi Ch'i-Kung
The Methods for Developing Ch'i and Breath
Fundamental procedures for strengthening the ch'i -
Reasons for practicing ch'i-kung - The benefits of ch'i-kung
- The twenty-one gestures of ch'i-kung.

Chapter Six: 139
Training Exercises
Essential Training Exercises for T'ai Chi Ch'uan
- How to extend the ch'i - The Post Stances of T'ai Chi -
Eight Post Stance postures - How to perform Tsai-Tui -
Commentary on training terminology.

Index 161

Translator's Introduction

The main emphasis of this volume of the Chen Kung Series is to provide a foundation for the practice of T'ai Chi Ch'uan. Ideally, anyone beginning their T'ai Chi Ch'uan career would start with the fundamentals explained in this book.

Too many T'ai Chi-*ists* have to more or less backtrack in their studies. They first learn the form and later seek out the more fundamental exercises and principles. It would be well for the T'ai Chi Ch'uan community to consider this problem carefully. How many T'ai Chi-*ists* really understand, or can actually apply the necessary fundamentals of *sung* (alert relaxation), the one breath, mind-intent, sinking ch'i into the tan-tien and adhering ch'i to the spine?

Too often T'ai Chi Ch'uan is practiced and viewed as some sort of external gymnastic. T'ai Chi Ch'uan is an "internal art". Master T. T. Liang always advises, "In your practice only ten-percent is expressed externally, ninety-percent is unseen, internal." The majority of movement occurs inside, not outside. Yang Cheng-fu stated, "T'ai Chi Ch'uan is meditation in action, action within meditation." Abiding by the tan-tien is not an external activity; it is purely internal. An expanded and gracious looking form of T'ai Chi Ch'uan is not necessarily T'ai Chi Ch'uan.

Hopefully this book, as well as the additional volumes, will provide a better understanding of these fundamentals and principles which in turn will internalize your T'ai Chi Ch'uan to a greater degree. I think there will be something here for both the beginning and advanced T'ai Chi-*ist*. Much of the material I have left alone, without comment. Either it is something to be dealt with more fully in future volumes or it is something the students will discover for themselves. After all, this book is about practice and without practice the words are sterile. Practice will reveal a great deal to the reader.

T'ai Chi Ch'i-Kung

This is the focal exercise of this volume, which concentrates on learning to mobilize movement from breath, ch'i and mind-intent. This is usually a major breakthrough for most students, as beginners use the muscles to move their arms. However, in this exercise the arms, after continuous practice, in a sense float through the form.

Many of my students really praise this short, powerful exercise. However, I don't think it wise to promise too much in the way of ch'i development to those who only read this book, without seeking a genuine teacher who can recognize and thus help avert their particular obstacles or difficulties.

T'ai Chi translates as "supreme ultimate" and is used in the name to show that it belongs to the T'ai Chi Ch'uan system. *Ch'i-Kung* means "to work the breath and/or ch'i." There are various forms and practices of ch'i-kung. Some accentuate the external and others the internal. This exercise is internal ch'i-kung.

Natural vs. Reverse Breathing

Natural Breath: The abdomen expands on the inhalation and contracts on the exhalation.

Reverse Breath: The abdomen contracts on the inhalation and expands on the exhalation.

This T'ai Chi Ch'i-Kung form can be practiced with either of these methods of breathing. However, on the advice of Master Liang it is decidedly better to practice the natural breathing method. He claims that reverse breathing, if practiced incorrectly, has the tendency to rapidly produce negative ch'i, which can possibly create many psychological disorders, such as: anger, greed, sexual disorders and so forth.

Reverse breathing can be useful for a martial art. It is untrue, however, that it can help reverse the aging process. Reversing the aging process has to do first with tranquility. With reverse breathing tranquility is difficult to achieve. Under the guidance of a genuine teacher, however, reverse breathing can be very effective and useful.

Since I deal with natural breathing at length in my book **The Inner Court of T'ai Chi Ch'uan**, I will only discuss some of the basics here. The first rule of natural breathing is just that, to be natural. Do not force the breath to be either long, or deep. Let this happen naturally through practice. Use the mind-intent to keep the breath in the lower abdomen. Use the abdomen like a balloon or bellows — expand and contract it equally. Do not just push out the front of the stomach on inhalation and pull it inward on exhalation. Rather, on inhalation you should sense the breath on the lower spine, sides and front of the abdomen. On the exhalation, you should feel the contraction in a similar manner.

The Text

If the popularity of this work in the original Chinese text were measured against all other T'ai Chi Ch'uan writings published in China, then without question Chen Yen-lin's *T'ai Chi Ch'uan Tao Chien Kan San-Shou Ho Lun* (T'ai Chi Ch'uan, Sword, Sabre, Staff and Dispersing-Hands Combined) is the most widely read and distributed work on T'ai Chi Ch'uan throughout Asia. His book is literally the "T'ai Chi Ch'uan Bible" for the Yang style of T'ai Chi Ch'uan.

There are two reasons for its enormous popularity: 1) The book's materials are considered to be derived from the Yang family personal transcripts. 2) No matter what the source, the information presented shows a greater depth and insight into both the philosophy and practice of T'ai Chi Ch'uan than any other available work.

Given these two points I was amazed when I first read the book to discover that it had never before been made available to the English reader or T'ai Chi-*ist*. It was in 1982 that I first received a copy of this work from Master Tung-tsai Liang. In 1986 I had finished translating the bulk of the material. Master Liang helped with some of the more difficult terminology. During this same year I published the first edition of **Cultivating the Ch'i** and **T'ai Chi Sword, Sabre and Staff**, both of which sold out within a year. This is the second edition which has been completely revised, with numeric footnotes, photographs and graphics added for greater clarity.

The translation work produced five volumes in all. Briefly, the other volumes are:

• **The Intrinsic Energies of T'ai Chi Ch'uan** (Vol. Two): An in depth definition of the twenty-five intrinsic energies that can be developed within T'ai Chi Ch'uan.

• **The Original Yang Style of T'ai Chi Ch'uan** (Vol. Three): Contains materials on the origins and history of T'ai Chi Ch'uan, Yang family biographies, posture and application instruction, fundamental principles of practice and the T'ai Chi Ch'uan treatises and songs.

• **San-Shou, Tui-Shou and Ta-Lu of T'ai Chi Ch'uan** (Vol. Four): In depth explanation of the three primary two-person exercises.

• **T'ai Chi Sword, Sabre and Staff** (Vol. Five): Form instructions on the three weapons of T'ai Chi Ch'uan, introductory materials and related odes.

This particular portion of the Chen Kung series contains many Taoist alchemical terms. I have provided brief definitions of them for the most part. The problem with many of these terms is that they can be defined in various stages of reality. For example, *ching* can be defined as "sperm" on a physical substance level; as "regenerative force" on a primal energy level; and as "essence of transformation" on a spiritual level.

Another problem is the various terms used by the different schools of Taoism for the same thing, i.e., *tan-tien* has over two-hundred and sixty other terms to describe it. The largest problem however is that to fully understand many of the ideas which these terms represent, one needs to have some knowledge of Yin-Yang theory and Five Element theory, which permeate Taoist philosophy. However, fortunately, one does not need all this theory in order to practice the exercises. Therefore, I feel confident that my brief definitions will suffice.

During the translation work itself I was most fortunate to have been living with Master Liang, who helped greatly by sharing his wisdom in T'ai Chi Ch'uan. He gave me numerous insights into the specialized terms used throughout the text. I especially valued his help knowing that Master Liang's own book, **T'ai Chi Ch'uan For Health and Self-Defense** has the same stature with the English and Chinese reader as Chen's book. His small book has been extremely popular in America and Europe for fifteen years. Even in my travels to China, Hong Kong, Taiwan and Indonesia I frequently came across pirated copies of his work. Curiously, these thefts did not upset him; instead he expressed gratitude that people respected his work enough to pirate it in the first place.

We hope that the reader is already familiar with Master Liang's book or will become so. Much background material is presented there which relates to this work, such as the Yang family biographies, history of T'ai Chi Ch'uan and very insightful commentaries on the T'ai Chi Ch'uan treatises.

History of the Text

Sometime during the years 1929 to 1930, Chen Yen-lin, a rich merchant and student of Yang Cheng-fu, asked to borrow the family transcripts for just one evening so that he might read them to enhance his practice. Chen had been a loyal and dedicated student, so Yang Cheng-fu consented, knowing full well that in one night it would be difficult for even a fast reader to finish the book. What Yang Cheng-fu did not know was that Chen Yen-lin had hired seven transcribers to work through the night to copy the entire work.

Later in 1932 these notes appeared in book form and enjoyed rapid sales throughout China. This infuriated the Yang family, who then released a smaller book claiming that Chen's publication was a forgery and that their new smaller book was the genuine material. Chen, in typical Chinese style, claimed the book contained his own theories and that he only used the Yang family name for authenticity. This is Chinese politics at its best.

Master Liang told me this story. He in turn heard it through his teacher Cheng Man-ch'ing, who heard it from Yang Cheng-fu, his teacher. With this kind of oral testimony it would definitely be best not to make too many assumptions about the exactness of dates or the truth about how the materials were procured. However, in 1978, when Master Jou Tsung-hwa located Chen Yen-lin in Shanghai, Chen apparently confirmed the story.

Before anyone accuses Chen of any wrong doing, it is clear that the T'ai Chi Ch'uan world owes him a great debt, whatever the ethics or politics that were involved. The Yang family teachings might well have remained hidden or become lost; likewise, the Yang family might not have published the various works of their own. An even greater result was that many masters, for various reasons, began publishing their works also. Chen's courage created a chain reaction of teachers going public with their knowledge.

There is no question that Chen's hand played a role in the formation of the book, but it is doubtful, considering his lack of education, age and time spent learning T'ai Chi Ch'uan that he could have composed the work entirely on his own. Likewise, it is even less probable that Yang Cheng-fu was the original author. It is more probable that the bulk of the material, especially the section on intrinsic energies, was compiled by a disciple of Yang Lu-chan, the founder of Yang style and grandfather to Yang Cheng-fu. This disciple was Wu Ho-ching, who is also suspected of creating the T'ai Chi Ch'uan treatises in conjunction with Yang Lu-chan. For the sake of acceptance he attributed those treatises to the Ming Dynasty immortal, Chang San-feng.

Chen Yen-lin

Chen Yen-lin used the name Chen Kung as author of the book in question. He is also known in the West as Yearning K. Chen. Chen Yen-lin (1906 —) provides no background information about himself in his book. His explanations of intrinsic energies (*chin*) had never before appeared in any T'ai Chi Ch'uan related books, which really created an enigma about him. In 1980 Master Jou Tsung-hwa met with him in Shanghai and reports that Chen started T'ai Chi Ch'uan at age four and is now a doctor of Chinese medicine. This means that around age twenty-four to twenty-six he acquired the Yang family materials and published them. It can only be surmised that after his disappearance (around 1932) he changed professions from merchant to doctor of Chinese medicine.

In 1947 an English book titled **T'ai Chi Ch'uan: Its Effects and Practical Applications** appeared from Willow Pattern Press in Shanghai. The book lists Yearning K. Chen as the author and Kuo-shui Chang as translator. The interesting thing about this particular book is that it is not derived from the original Chinese version of Chen's work. The chapters on physics, psychology and morality probably derived from Cheng Man-ch'ing's **T'ai Chi Ch'uan Thirteen Treatises**. The solo form instructions and practical application explanations are similar, but not identical by any means. So whether or not this book is by Chen Yen-lin is unclear. But what is clear is that it is not taken from the material presented here.

The Translation

The original text is somewhat organized, at least in the placement of the chapters. The difficulty in translation, however, was the sporadic placement of certain sentences within the chapters, which was literally "Oh, by the way, *this* and *that* should be…" I have corrected the positions of these sentences.

Another difficulty was in specialized terms, where the Yang family invents characters for their own purposes or applies a variant meaning unlike common usage. Take for example, an invented character like *lu*. *Lu* in common usage means to "pull-back", which is actually how many T'ai Chi Ch'uan texts present it. However, by placing *shou* as the main radical, we have a depiction of motion. This then becomes "*roll-back*", as it is the hand which turns over to the back; there is not a "pulling."

An example of a variant meaning is *tsou*, which is usually translated as "to walk" or "to travel", but in connection with T'ai Chi Ch'uan the Yang family gave it the meaning of "*to receive*". There are numerous other examples of this throughout the body of the text. I mention these difficulties in part to illustrate that the original composer of this work was not merely an expert T'ai Chi-*ist*, but would have to have been quite educated in the literary realm of the Chinese language.

Another difficult aspect, particularly in this volume, is the abundance of Taoist alchemy terms, many of which are not commonly found even in popular Taoist works published in China, especially the meditation terms found in Chapter Four. Likewise, to perform the Small Heavenly Circuits in the manner described would require that someone be steeped in Taoist alchemical terminology and practices.

After having completed my translation I could draw only one conclusion, that the first two volumes (**Cultivating the Ch'i** and **The Intrinsic Energies of T'ai Chi Ch'uan**) were definitely not authored by Chen Yen-lin or Yang Cheng-fu. Again, it is more probable that these were derived from Yang Lu-chan's wisdom and experiences with the literary skills applied by his scholar-disciple Wu Ho-ching. If correct, these writings become ever-the-more valuable to the present day T'ai Chi-*ist*.

The Graphics

Chen Yen-lin notes at the end of the book that all the drawings within the text may be incorrect, containing many errors. In the case of the T'ai Chi Ch'i-Kung exercise drawings there are many minor errors and one major. The feet must be separated at shoulder width so that the ch'i can flow freely through the buttocks and coccyx region. If performed with the heels together this entire area would be obstructed.

It is interesting that Yang Cheng-fu is used as the model for all the drawings other than those for the T'ai Chi Ch'i-Kung exercise. Who the model is for these, or if there was one, is unknown. Concerning the other drawings for which Yang Cheng-fu is the model, it is relatively easy to determine their origin. In 1925 a book titled, **T'ai Chi Ch'uan Techniques** by disciple Chen Wei-ming (no relation to Chen Yen-lin) appeared with thirty-seven photographs of Cheng-fu performing T'ai Chi Ch'uan postures and four performing Pushing-Hands (Tui-Shou) with disciple Hsu Yu-sheng. The book was not widely distributed until around 1934. However, Chen Yen-lin would certainly have had access to it in order to complete the other drawings. In his 1947 English work, Chen credits a Mr. Pao-hua for the graphics. Chen obviously used the photgraphs which appeared in Chen Wei-ming's book as his models. This still leaves the question of the origins of the T'ai Chi Ch'i-Kung drawings.

In light of the errors in those drawings, we took new photographs of myself to make the postures more readily understandable. For authenticity's sake, however, the original drawings are included at the end of Chapter Five. Those drawings relating to Chapter Six are presented in the same way. All the other graphics I included to make the exercises and text more understandable.

Summaries of the Chapters

The chapters presented within this volume are not just directed at the practice of T'ai Chi Ch'i-Kung. Ultimately they are meant to be the foundation for all the practices of T'ai Chi Ch'uan. Within these chapters there is a progression of learning and, depending on the quality of practice, a development of ch'i.

The first four chapters appear here just as they do in the original text. However, the last two chapters (Five and Six) were originally placed after a lengthy explanation of intrinsic energies (which is the body of Vol. Two). Chapter Six is composed of pieces placed either before or after the T'ai Chi Ch'i-Kung exercise explanation. With Master Liang's advice, I feel that the placement of these materials is now much more organized than that of the original text.

Chapter One: *T'ai Chi Ch'uan and Nourishing-Life*

The purpose of the chapter is mainly to encourage people to practice any of the kungs of T'ai Chi Ch'uan so they might enjoy a healthy life even in old age. The material covers a wide range of concepts associated with the practice of T'ai Chi Ch'uan, all of which provide what the Taoists term *Yang-Sheng,* or Nourishing-Life.

The Taoist concept of Nourishing-Life, in essence, is to develop the ching, ch'i and shen (The Three Treasures), which in turn can be called *"guarding the One"* or *"abiding by the tan-tien."* This "abiding by the tan-tien" is accomplished through mind-intent and ch'i.

Chapter Two: *Discourse on Mind-Intent and Ch'i*

The most important piece of information being related here is that mind-intent and ch'i are mutually dependent. This is a point well explained in this chapter. Indeed, on the level of importance, this chapter outweighs the rest. Too many people practice T'ai Chi Ch'uan with the idea that breathing low in the abdomen will somehow produce ch'i. The practitioner might gain a little benefit from this, but will certainly not achieve what is called "*bright ch'i*", more likely a negative ch'i called "*scorching heat*".

Many ill-informed Ch'i-Kung practitioners, East and West, have suffered the ill effects of not understanding, or not having been taught, how to properly abide by the tan-tien; how to properly develop mind-intent; and how to internally train "the one breath". This chapter provides the correct information for these practices.

Chapter Three: *Internal Breathing Methods for Mobilizing the Ch'i*

From understanding the mind-intent and ch'i, the ch'i must be mobilized. This chapter explains the stages of *upper* and *lower* level breath, its relation to *hsien t'ien ch'i* and *hou t'ien ch'i* and how these two mutually mobilize each other. It further explains how the *heng ha* sounds work to stimulate ch'i and to lay the foundation for tranquility. There is also a discussion on how these methods are applied in two-person drills.

Chapter Four: *T'ai Chi Ch'uan and Meditation*

This chapter surprised me when I first translated it because the methods for visualizing points, or cavities, are very old, from a Ming Dynasty sect of Taoism. In present times the Small Heavenly Circuit was what this text refers to as hsien t'ien ch'i and hou t'ien ch'i. The Small Heavenly Circuits (commonly called Microcosmic Orbit) here take place in the *Upper Tan-Tien* (head and neck area); *Middle Tan-Tien* (between chest and navel); and the *Lower Tan-Tien* (navel and lower abdomen area). These are very effective methods for stimulating ch'i, and should be approached in stages.

Chapter Five: *T'ai Chi Ch'i-Kung*

Herein are the directions for performing the twenty-one posture T'ai Chi Ch'i-Kung. Externally this is a very easy exercise to learn. The difficult aspect of the exercise is the application of mind-intent and ch'i so that you perform it with the "one breath".

Each posture's instructional text has on its opposite page a large photograph of myself demonstrating the full motion of the posture. All twenty-one movements should be strung together smoothly and evenly, unless a slight pause is called for in the instructional material.

Chapter Six: *Training Exercises*

The first of these supplemental exercises is to *Extend or Express the Ch'i*, in a shaking motion. But the motion is to be felt more internally, feeling the energy from tan-tien, up the spine, into the arms and out the finger tips. This will help balance the energy in your body, for too many t'ai chi-*ists* concentrate only on accumulation of ch'i, not on the expression of it.

The second exercise, *Standing Post Horse Stance*, is primarily a breathing exercise and secondarily a standing meditation. Again, treat this exercise as you would T'ai Chi Ch'i-Kung. All the same principles apply. Also, be patient, starting with one, a few minutes each day. Progress cautiously and with discretion.

The third exercise, *Ch'uan Tzu*, is in essence a standing meditation. The key to these exercises is not in making the legs strong (in a muscular sense), but to apply *sung* (relaxation). When feeling the legs tense, mentally let the tension go. After a long, continued period of letting go, the legs will become softer and more relaxed.

The fourth set of exercises are *The Eight Postures of Ch'uang Pu*, which are the eight primary postures of T'ai Chi Ch'uan. Some teachers profess that standing post stances are performed to make the legs strong. This is only partially true. The real strength comes from *sung*, not from exertion of muscles, as there must be a constant letting go of tension in the legs.

The fifth exercise, *Tsai-Tui*, has many facets. The importance of this exercise lies in unifying the body so as to express the ch'i in the limbs simultaneously. Again, it is relatively easy to perform, but difficult to master internally.

The above five exercises should be practiced daily. But first study the text thoroughly so you have a good understanding of not only purpose, but the functions as well. Do not be overly anxious, take your time by exercising them a little each day, building up gradually to make more repetitions.

Conclusion

When I first asked Master Liang to teach me the T'ai Chi Ch'i-Kung exercises he refused, saying that "This is to cast pearls before a swine," an old Chinese idiom meaning, don't give things to someone who cannot understand and appreciate their value. I always loved his seemingly endless storehouse of such idioms. But I decided that this was an exercise worth learning so I translated the entire section and proceeded to teach myself.

Feeling proud after having learned the entire sequence, I got him to sit and watch me, hoping I could get his approval or advice. After finishing I asked for his opinion. He got a big smile on his face and said, "Beautiful!" (pause) "What *it is?*" Later he told me that I must translate other sections in order to get the principles of the exercises.

A few months later and after careful study I showed him again. This time I got a very disgruntled look, at which point he said, "You are more dangerous than an atomic bomb!" My feeling was that I had failed, not only in translating the materials correctly, but also that I failed in patience by so boldly taking on the task of teaching myself.

A few weeks later, however, we had guests staying at the house who wanted to learn T'ai Chi Ch'uan. The evening they had arrived, Master Liang came downstairs to greet them. Abruptly he questioned them, "What do you want to learn from me?" Startled, one said, "Anything you would like to teach us sir." He then turned to me and commanded, "Teach them T'ai Chi Ch'i-Kung, but if you don't do it correctly you will get fifty slashes."

With a note of humor and sarcasm I responded, "But you said I was an atomic bomb. How can I teach?"

"You bloody!" he said glaringly, "I said you were as dangerous as an atomic bomb. That's different. From now on I must be careful what books I lend you. If you steal all my art then I'll have no defense! That's an atomic bomb!"

Later on Master Liang explained how he used to train in T'ai Chi Ch'i-Kung in Taiwan, doing so for about ten years. He further explained that it is a marvelous exercise, but that at a certain point in your development you will no longer need it. He added a cute quip, "Just like Chen Kung says in his book, I can now live off my savings account. You, young man, are a spendthrift!" Indeed I am. Seven years since learning T'ai Chi Ch'i-Kung I'm still striving to save.

Winter, 1991
Stuart Alve Olson

Cultivating
the Ch'i

One
T'ai Chi Ch'uan and
Nourishing-Life[1]

You can use each of the boxing exercises[2] to refine and discipline[3] your body and mind. You can mobilize and stimulate the spirit of vitality[4] which will then flow like water, rather than remaining stagnant. It will be like a door pivot which never becomes worm-eaten.

There are numerous styles of Chinese boxing with truly ancient histories and origins. On the external level, there are those who favor the hard styles, and those who favor the soft styles.

Different generations have regarded the Shaolin Ch'uan energies as mere external displays emphasizing only that which is unyielding; they have regarded the T'ai Chi Ch'uan energies as only a collection of internal imaginings, emphasizing only that which is yielding. They do not understand that the highest skill of Shaolin Ch'uan is the combination of the unyielding and the yielding.

An error that occurs with those who favor only hard styles is that the feet and legs lean in all the movements; they do not realize that leaning will obstruct the ch'i.[7]

T'ai Chi Ch'uan primarily develops soft skin and flesh; the skin and flesh are soft like cotton, yet the internal ch'i is strong, like iron of superior quality. This is called, *"An iron bar wrapped in silk or cotton."* [8]

It is really immaterial what school or style you practice, as you should not give undue attention to either hardness or softness. Just make sure the main principles are not neglected, even momentarily. Focus entirely on whatever vehicle is being made use of to acquire skill.

When practicing T'ai Chi Ch'uan, you may form the habit of being too soft and yielding[9]. There really is no advantage in this. You will become lethargic and sluggish. Students should be aware of the advantages of the fundamental principles, practicing the movements slowly and evenly, inhaling and exhaling naturally so as to accumulate ch'i and concentrate the *shen* (spirit), without employing muscular strength too excessively. It is through softness and gentleness that you achieve mastery. This softness and gentleness means soft and continuous movements in accordance with harmonious breathing.

Ching, ch'i, shen and the intrinsic energies are all to be brought to their full capacity. Neither the internal nor external aspects of these energies should be based entirely on the kind of softness and gentleness that leads to lethargy or immobility. This is central to *tui-shou* (pushing-hands), where brute-force[10] is strong, but cannot exist for long; and intrinsic energy likewise cannot be totally devoid of strength.

Consider the expression "Removing one thousand catties with only four ounces." This is to have the skillful energy[11] of four ounces. Attempting to remove one thousand catties with only brute-force, without the intrinsic energy of four ounces is impossible. How can this be done?

Through slowness you can later be soft; through evenness you can later be gentle. The capability of being soft and gentle will cause the muscle and bone to be opened. The ch'i and blood will circulate harmoniously. From this the breath will become deep and long and the spirit of vitality (ching shen) can be stimulated and brought forth.

If you suffer in old age from such serious illnesses as consumption, heart disease, high blood pressure, or numbness in the extremities you should take up these exercises.

By practicing T'ai Chi Ch'uan you can completely cure the insufficiencies of the *hsien t'ien* (before heaven) and repair injuries to the *hou t'ien* (after heaven)[12]. So if possible when you are still young and able-bodied enough you should devote yourself entirely to continuous practice, without interruption. As a result you will obtain not only a lifetime of benefit, but a life worth writing about.

FU HSI
DIAGRAM
"BEFORE HEAVEN"

During your youth, your stamina[13] is more than sufficient to handle strenuous work and to accomplish tasks with relative speed. If you become physically vigorous and robust by practicing T'ai Chi Ch'uan in the years that you are naturally able-bodied, then in old age you can succeed in illuminating your spirit and in the completion of bright ch'i; every movement will be light and nimble; there will be no affliction of the waist and no back pain; no withering of the spirit of vitality, or anxious breathing and groaning, which are symptoms of disease.

These types of conditions are quite similar to that of saving money, because in our youth we can also save our bodies through discipline and refinement, like a daily accumulation of virtue. Then in old age we can enjoy and use this. Daily

KING WEN DIAGRAM
"AFTER HEAVEN"

accumulation is of no further concern. Otherwise in a moment of crisis there is nothing to fall back on. People of different generations have not really understood this viewpoint. For the most part, there are two views concerning this matter:

During youth the energy is strong and the body does not normally suffer many illnesses. So what advantage is there in disciplining and refining the body?

There are those who practice these *kungs*[14] for only a while, then think they can dispense with their practice. However, in their old age, as they approach death, they will suffer bitterly because they no longer practice.

How can anyone possibly know beforehand that these two viewpoints are utterly erroneous? Because young people have strong and vital bodies, with the ch'i functioning more than satisfactorily, they certainly do not see the beneficial outcome of disciplining and refining the body and mind. When reaching old age, on the other hand, the ch'i weakens. At this time, to your regret, your resistance is not sufficient internally, and you suffer when you reach the point of death. The experience of those who practice these kungs and have these conditions will be exactly the opposite.

T'ai Chi Ch'uan bases itself exclusively on gentleness, softness, naturalness and bringing you back to your original nature. Daily training makes the muscles and bones become softer and more pliable, and it especially causes the breath to become natural. These are the results of disciplining and refining the ching, ch'i and shen to the end of your days. How then can you consider dispensing with your kung or wish to suffer bitterly?

The old masters of T'ai Chi Ch'uan, in days gone by, would very often sit cross-legged, smile and then die. This is evidence that they found the two previous viewpoints to be erroneous. For others who practice T'ai Chi Ch'uan it would be satisfying enough to just attain a peaceful death.

When practicing the postures of T'ai Chi Ch'uan you should seek to be correct and not rely on brute-force. You must be centered, calm and composed.

Embrace the Origin and Guard the One [15], without thought and without anxiety. Take every opportunity to practice.

Pay attention and make the entire body comfortable. If, after a while you become weary, rest. Should the practice periods be long or short? Who can know completely each individual's energy? It is not necessary to be too ambitious or too tied to old conventions concerning practice. But those who do constantly practice can endure because they hold it in such high esteem. If this is the case and you are able to train constantly, then in the course of time you will certainly acquire the benefits of practice.

In your beginnning practice, you may not have the necessary motivation to work the blood and ch'i. But in the blink of an eye *the flag is seen*[16] and the entire interior is strengthened. The ch'i will function fully, the "hundred illnesses" will be eliminated and vitality and health preserved intact.

Therefore, seek out the Way of Nourishing-Life with the practice of this orthodox art of T'ai Chi Ch'uan. But above all rely on yourself to generate effective results.

CHAPTER ONE NOTES

1. **YANG-SHENG:** *Nourishing-Life.* In the simplest form yang-sheng means "to beget life." But in Taoism it is a generic term denoting the idea of cultivating the vital essences, ching, ch'i and shen. Normally yang-sheng is a reference to hygiene practices, such as T'ai Chi Ch'uan, Ch'i-Kung and Tao-Yin. However, in the Taoist sense, yang-sheng is divided into eight branches of practice: 1) *Ching Tso* (meditation practice), 2) *Tao Yin* (guiding and directing ch'i flow) 3) *T'u Na* (purifying techniques of the breath), 4) *Fu Erh* (ingesting herbs and medicines), 5) *Fu Ch'i* (preserving energy and breath), 6) *Lien Ch'i* (regulating the ch'i), 7) *Pi Ku* (abstaining from grains), 8) *Fang Chung Shu* (inner chamber arts).

An ancient Taoist ode says,
"Hearing the sound of flowing water nourishes the ears;
Seeing the green of trees and plants nourishes the eyes;
Studying books which explain principles nourishes the mind;
Playing the lute and practicing writing nourishes the fingers;
Wandering about on foot with a staff nourishes the feet;
Tranquility of mind and sitting in meditation nourishes the nature;
Harmonizing the breath and ch'i nourishes the muscles and sinews."

2. Meaning, the solo form of T'ai Chi Ch'uan, as well as T'ai Chi Ch'i- Kung, San-Shou, Ta-Lu, T'ai Chi Sword, T'ai Chi Sabre and T'ai Chi Staff. Any and all the practices of the T'ai Chi Ch'uan system are vehicles in themselves for Nourishing-Life.

3. **TUAN LIEN:** *Refinement and Discipline. Tuan* means to "forge metal", hence the idea of discipline. *Lien* means to "smelt," thus the notion of refinement. The Taoists normally use this metallurgical analogy to explain the internal alchemical process, of taking raw ore and through the forging and smelting processes, acquiring pure steel. Hence, in Taoist forms the idea is discipline (*forge*) the ching, refine (*smelt*) the ch'i, and in the end obtain pure spirit (*pure steel*).

4. **CHING SHEN:** *Spirit of Vitality.* A term denoting the essential nature of a person, which is namely, ching, ch'i and shen.

5. This is referring to not only branches of T'ai Chi Ch'uan (Chen

Style, Yang Style, Wu Style — the most popular of the schools), but Shaolin Temple systems, Pa-Kua Chang and Hsing-I Ch'uan as well.

6. **CHIN:** *Intrinsic Energy.* Even though both schools, that of Shaolin and T'ai Chi Ch'uan have the development of martial skills called intrinsic energies (chin), Shaolin Ch'uan relies more heavily on *li* (strength), whereas T'ai Chi Ch'uan focuses on energy developing out of *sung* (sensitivity, awareness, relaxation and intuition in combination).

7. Extreme bending of joints obstructs blood flow, as does leaning the legs (knees over the toes), which likewise obstructs not only the circulation of internal ch'i, but intrinsic energy (chin) as well.

8. In brief, this is a result of the ch'i penetrating the bone, turning it into marrow (*the iron bar*), and the effect of sung on the muscles, sinews and tendons (*silk or cotton*).

9. Becoming too soft and yielding means, as Master T.T. Liang explains, "Becoming so relaxed that you are in a state of collapse. T'ai Chi Ch'uan is an external appearance of relaxation, but internally one is very sensitive and alert."

10. **CHO-LI:** *Brute-Force.* Literally, clumsy and unskilled strength.

11. **CH'IAO CHIN:** *Skilful Energy.* The opposite of brute-force. This is acquired through the practice of the correct principles of the boxing art in which you train.

12. **HSIEN T'IEN and HOU T'IEN:** *Before Heaven* and *After Heaven.* A Taoist concept expressing many aspects of self-cultivation and philosophy. For example:
- Hsien t'ien represents inhalation, and hou t'ien exhalation.
- Hsien t'ien is the spirit of vitality (ching shen) ascending upwards from the spine; hou t'ien is the ching shen descending down the front of the body.
- Hsien t'ien also is represented in Fu Hsi's arrangement of the Eight Diagrams, and hou t'ien by King Wen's arrangement of the Eight

Diagrams.
- Hsien t'ien is often used to mean "reverse breathing" and hou t'ien, "natural breathing."

The philosophy of Hsien T'ien and Hou T'ien is very broad and abstruse, equal to that of the Five Element theory and Yin-Yang theory — all of which interconnect and for the most part form the basis of Chinese philosophy in general.

Insufficiency of the hsien t'ien means that one has not conserved ching, accumulated ch'i or congealed the shen, which can be accomplished through the correct practice of T'ai Chi Ch'uan. Hence the hsien t'ien will be complete, which is a restoration of one's original state (before heaven or before birth). Some also translate this as pre-natal breath (hsien t'ien ch'i) and post-natal breath (hou t'ien ch'i).

Repair injuries of the hou t'ien means that once the hsien t'ien is restored the essences (ching, ch'i and shen) can be refined (ching), stimulated (ch'i) and issued (shen), which heals and prevents all physical and spiritual ills.

So "curing insufficiencies and repairing injuries" through hsien t'ien and hou t'ien is a reference directed at nourishing-life and immortality as well.

13. **CHING-LI:** *Stamina.* Because during youth your ching is not yet damaged or injured through excessive dissipation, you still have sufficient physical and mental strength.

14. **KUNG:** This is a generic term meaning the "energy applied to a task." It is also used to describe the ideas of "effort, work, skill and merit." Herein, kung is used to mean the exercises of T'ai Chi Ch'uan.

15. **PAO YUAN:** *Embrace the Origin,* and **SHOU-I:** *Guard the One.* Both of these terms mean the same thing. They are the very essence of all Taoist self-cultivation practices. In T'ai Chi Ch'uan specifically they mean, "to abide by the tan-tien," and "sink the ch'i into the tan-tien," which is the central focus of internal self-cultivation.

16. *The flag is seen* is an analogy taken from **The Mental Elucidation of the Thirteen Kinetic Postures**, a T'ai Chi Ch'uan treatise, attributed to the immortal Wang Chung-yueh of the Ming Dynasty. It says: "*The mind is the commander; the ch'i is the flag; the waist is the banner.*" So, seeing the flag means that you realize and experience the ch'i. You will then want to completely devote yourself to practice.

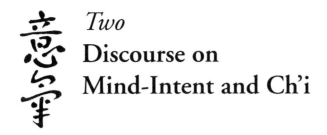

Two
Discourse on
Mind-Intent and Ch'i

Within each person there is *mind-intent* [1] and ch'i [2], both of which are invisible and formless.

It is essential to know that the ch'i is produced within the body. To harness this energy is extremely important as the ch'i and the body must satisfy each other's needs.

In application, the ch'i stimulates the blood and nourishes it. This is the process of perfecting the ch'i. The heat from the ch'i rises up from the *"gate of life."* [3] The *ching* [4] should then be cherished and nourished. Both of these (the ch'i and ching) should be repeatedly stimulated and perfected. The Taoist schools call this, *"perfecting the fire and water,"* [5] or the *"internal elixir."* They seek to retain the ch'i and store it in the *tan-tien* [6]. The Taoists regard the ch'i as being an exceptionally precious possession.

Blood or ch'i, what is to be most prized? Most people are unaware that the ch'i is more substantial than the blood. The ch'i acts as the master to the blood; the blood is like the assistant.

The ch'i is like the troops and the blood like the camp. During a man's entire lifetime he must depend completely upon both the troops and the camp. Supposing an army had a camp and no troops; there would then be no convoys. Likewise, having troops and no camp, there would be nowhere to unite.

In other words, the ch'i is most important and the blood is
secondary. If the blood is insufficient, it is still possible to
maintain life for a short period, but if the ch'i is lacking, there
will arise an immediate crisis, resulting in death.

Therefore, when nourishing the ch'i, what is the most important
condition? Specifically you must practice T'ai Chi Ch'uan. Get
rid of the external gymnastics. Moreover, master the production
and nourishment of ch'i. As the proverb says, "Externally
exercise the muscles, bones and skin; internally train the one
breath."[7] So in general this means to practice T'ai Chi Ch'uan.

It becomes immaterial later on whether you practice the circular
motions of the solo forms, the *tui-shou* [8] or the *ta-lu* [9] exercises.
All that really matters is that while performing these exercises
you are conscious of breathing naturally. Likewise, your facial
expression should be unchanging.

The ch'i should circulate throughout the inner areas of the body.
Previous to stretching and before actually having set the exercise
into motion, you will already be well aware of how to nourish
the ch'i through the exercises. The efficacy of the T'ai Chi
Ch'uan exercises is very great. So on no account corrupt your
practice by training in too hasty, laborious or fatiguing a
manner. This cannot be stressed enough.

When the blood has been completely purified, the body will
become extremely strong. When the body is strong the mind is
strengthened and rendered more determined. With this the
spirit (*p'o*)[10] is made strong and brave. With a strong spirit you
can increase your life span and benefit greatly from this longer
life.

Students should know that the only gateway to acquiring the
skills of T'ai Chi Ch'uan is by constant cultivation of ch'i.

Some have said that mind-intent is no other than the mind (rational thinking), or that the mind is no other than the mind-intent. But truly there is both a mind and mind-intent; they are two separate things and should be thought of as such.

The master of the mind is the mind-intent. The mind acts as only an assistant to the mind-intent. When the mind moves, it does so because of the mind-intent; when the mind-intent arises the ch'i will follow.

In other words: mind, mind-intent and ch'i are all interconnected and work in a rotational manner. When the mind is confused the mind-intent will disperse. When the mind-intent is dispersed the ch'i will become insubstantial (weak).

So it is said, "*When the ch'i sinks into the tan-tien, the mind-intent is made strong and vital; with a strong and vital mind-intent, the mind then becomes tranquil.*" Therefore, these three mutually employ each other, and in truth they must be united and not allowed to become separate.

The application of ch'i will expedite the blood circulation and stimulate the spirit. When the spirit and ch'i circulation are active, they can then be put into use; otherwise, neither the ch'i nor the mind-intent can be regulated properly.

The way of the ch'uan (internal boxing) art is to have regulation without method, or principles without techniques. At some point this will be clear to the ch'uan-*ist.*

Having only techniques without principles amounts to nothing more than giving up one's capital in order to follow an inferior scheme (to invest in a losing business venture).

So, in the ch'uan arts, the regulation of ch'i and mind-intent is based on mutual dependence. But to actually employ mind-intent and the ch'i within your T'ai Chi Ch'uan practice is very, very difficult, especially for beginning students. Yet, there really is no beginning method other than practicing the thirteen postures of the solo movements.

What is absolutely necessary in the beginning, however, is to follow the imagination. For instance: when the two hands perform the *Press* gesture, there is an imagined intent to the front, as if an opponent was really there. At this time, within the palms of the hands there is no ch'i which can be issued. The practitioner must then imagine the ch'i rising up from the tan-tien into the spine, through the arms and into the wrists and palms. Thus, accordingly, the ch'i is imagined to have penetrated outwards onto the opponent's body.

This use of imagination during initial study and practice will be difficult to trust and will not be susceptible to proof. Only after a long period of training will you be able to apply it in a natural manner, which is when the ch'i penetrates the inner regions of the body. This occurs when the gestures maintain two circuits of the ch'i[11]; then the ch'i flows into the limbs of the body. When control of the mind-intent is achieved, the ch'i will follow. At what point this occurs is immaterial as long as it is mobilized.

In T'ai Chi Ch'uan there are the fundamental principles of "*opening* and *closing,*" "*fullness* and *emptiness,*" "*inhaling* and *exhaling*" and "*advancing* and *withdrawing.*" These are the training methods for circulating the ch'i throughout the entire body. From these the body will become quite sensitive and alert, as will the muscles and tendons. The sense of touch will also become increasingly more acute. Thus, the spirit will be made active and alert.

Within the text of **The Mental Elucidation of the Thirteen Kinetic Postures** there is a verse which states, "*If the ch'i is not* *present the spirit of vitality of the entire body and mind will be obstructed. When the ch'i is present there is no need to exert muscular force, and without the ch'i it is simply hardness."*

In summary, the ch'i will be useless unless it is dutifully regulated in an unconscious manner. Otherwise, the ch'i will cause obstructions in your body, become unstable or fleeting, or abruptly produce a state of anger. At the time of having to issue the ch'i, obstructive ch'i, unstable ch'i and anger ch'i will cause the feet to float and make the center of balance unsteady. This is what is meant to "be without strength."

T'ai Chi Ch'uan is said to center around the ch'i of the tan-tien, (positive ch'i). This ch'i is very pure and tranquil. This tranquility makes it possible to be harmonious; this harmony makes it lucid; and lucidity makes the ch'i safe and unobstructed. This prevents the ch'i from producing scorching heat. In no way is this type of ch'i similar to the above three negative kinds of ch'i.

The discussion on ch'i within the text of **The Mental Elucidation of the Thirteen Kinetic Postures** is of great importance. For example:

*The mind moves the ch'i so that it may sink
deeply and penetrate the bones. When the ch'i circulates freely and unhindered throughout the body,
then it can easily follow the intentions of the mind.*

The mind-intent and ch'i must interact in a lively manner in order to achieve both smoothness and circularity.

The ch'i is mobilized as though it were threading a pearl with nine crooked pathways; no hollow or corner is left unreached.

The ch'i should be nourished naturally so as
not to have any injurious effects.

Relax (sung) *the abdomen, to allow the ch'i to*
penetrate into the bones.

Whether moving 'to or fro' the ch'i is to adhere
to the spine.

Within **The Song of Thirteen Postures** it is said:

The ch'i should be circulated throughout the
entire body without the slightest obstruction.

When the mind-intent and ch'i are the rulers
the bones and flesh follow their dictates.

When the mind-intent and ch'i are regulated,
it follows that the bones and flesh will become
heavier.

These verses concerning the ch'i are all of great importance.
When learning these it is difficult to distinguish all of them from
one another, especially when differentiating bright (*positive*) ch'i
from the scorching heat of the obstructive (*negative*) ch'i.

The relationship between the mind-intent and ch'i is like that of
an automobile; inside is the driver and an engine. The mind-
intent is the driver and the ch'i, the engine. Either of these
would be seriously lacking without the other..

CHAPTER TWO NOTES

1. **I:** (pronounced *yi*) In the practice of T'ai Chi Ch'uan the function of the *mind-intent*, or will, is both transcendental and intrinsically connected with ch'i. Mind-intent is neither a conditioned response nor an unconscious reaction. It is a reaction founded in awareness, intuition and sensitivity. However, mind-intent is *"conditioned"* in that it is developed over a long period of time through practice of the various T'ai Chi Ch'uan exercises. The mind-intent is also *"unconcious"* in that the rational thinking mind is not used.

The problem in defining the mind-intent is an empirical one in that you must first be truly capable of sinking the ch'i into tan-tien, which then strengthens the vitality of mind-intent, which in turn will affect the mind, producing tranquility. So without initiating the use of mind-intent, however vague at first, in order to sink the ch'i into the tan-tien, the mind-intent cannot be made strong enough for you to truly realize the difference between mind-intent and mind.

2. **CH'I:** *Vital Life Energy and/or Breath.* There are many explanations of what ch'i is, such as: an inherent oxygen in the blood for stamina and vitality; or a subtle cosmic energy which constitutes life, growth and motion in all things. Both these, and all the explanations, are true. Most teachings and teachers however prefer to explain its stimulation, nourishment, accumulation and/or circulation, than to attempt the difficult task of defining it.

In T'ai Chi Ch'uan and seated meditation you experience the sensations of ch'i when 1) mind-intent sinks the ch'i into the tan-tien, 2) when mind-intent becomes vital, and 3) the mind is tranquil — then ch'i will not only be sensed, but will circulate freely throughout the entire body.

3. **MING-MEN:** *The Gate of Life.* This is a ch'i cavity associated with the kidneys, located over the kidneys along the spine.

4. **CHING:** *Regenerative Force or Energy.* Ching is usually translated as sperm (for the male) and sexual fluids (for women). However ching is not necessarily just a substance, but rather the subtle energy which produces it, i.e., sexual force or the force that gives all things form. All

Taoist practices call for the conservation of ching, which stimulates the ch'i, which stimulates shen (spirit). (For more information on this subject see **The Jade Emperor's Mind-Seal Classic: A Discourse on Refining the Three Treasures (Ching, Ch'i, Shen)**, translation and commentary by Stuart Alve Olson. Dragon Door Publications, 1992).

5. **HUO SHUI:** *Fire and Water.* A symbolic expression representing the interaction of ching and ch'i. The idea is that the ch'i heats the ching, which then causes the ch'i to move; once the ch'i moves and can be circulated this is then "perfecting the fire and water."

6. **TAN-TIEN:** *Field of Elixir.* This is the central and most important ch'i center of all Chinese spiritual practices. This center, or cavity, is the source from which the ch'i is stimulated and accumulated. In T'ai Chi Ch'uan all movement finds its source originating from the tan-tien. It is called the "field of elixir" because the Three Treasures (ching, ch'i and shen) are all united, forming a mixture in the central point (Taoist analogies: *pot, stove, furnace, caldron*) and are refined forming an elixir, which then confers health, longevity, immortality or enlightenment, depending upon the degree to which the essences (ching, ch'i and shen) have been refined.

The process with the tan-tien in T'ai Chi Ch'uan is as follows:

The mind-intent leads the ch'i down into the tan-tien; when this is accomplished the ch'i strengthens the mind-intent; the more vital the mind-intent, the greater the mobilization of ch'i and the greater the tranquility of the mind. At this point the entire body moves in accordance with the movement of ch'i guided by mind-intent. This is true spontaneity and *sung* (relaxation, alertness and sensitivity). This is why the T'ai Chi Ch'uan classics insist on *"abiding by the tan-tien"*.

If one were to strip Taoism to its bare essentials there would be nothing left except "abiding by the tan-tien" in order to concentrate the ching, ch'i and shen in *one* center. This is the root of all Taoist philosophy and practices; everything else is but branches and leaves. Lao Tzu (*Tao Te Ching*) says: "Embrace the One (*Pao-I*) and return to the source (*Kuei Yuan*)," which means abide by the tan-tien.

7. **I K'OU CH'I:** *In One Breath.* This means: with one mind focus and

concentrate on the internal. The term carries various meanings, ranging from: connecting the inhalation and exhalation without pause, one flowing into the next; developing the mind and body unceasingly so that both function as one unit; and completion (internal attainment), which is the result of continuous repetition of practice. Sometimes this term is given as *i-ch'i* (*one breath; one action; one energy*). Here, i k'ou chi, literally translates as "one mouthful of ch'i," which in the higher practices of Taoist alchemy is a reference to the ingesting of breath or swallowing ch'i.

8. **TUI-SHOU:** *Pushing-Hands.* This is one of the three main two-person training exercises of T'ai Chi Ch'uan concerning development of chin (intrinsic energy) and its application, both in fixed form and free-sparring. The other two are *san-shou* and *ta-lu.* Tui-shou is generally associated with the movements of the four initial postures of of *Ward-Off, Roll-Back, Press* and *Push.* (San-shou, *dispersing-hands,* is exclusive to Yang style T'ai Chi Ch'uan. San-shou is a two-person exercise dealing with the applications, in active stepping, of the postures of T'ai Chi Ch'uan. See following note for explanation of ta-lu).

9. **TA-LU:** *Great Roll-Back.* This exercise is associated with the movements of the four diagonal directions and the *Four Primary Postures* of Pull, Split, Elbow-Stroke and Shoulder-Stroke, which are neutralized by the postures of Ward-Off, Roll-Back, Push and Press. However, there are other variations of ta-lu besides this one.

10. **P'O:** *Earth Bound Spirit* or *Sentient Spirit.* In brief, Taoism professes that a person obtains two spirit energies at birth, the *p'o* and *h'un* (heavenly and earthly bound spirit). P'o represents the physical body; h'un the spiritual body. Now, at the time of death, if the Three Treasures are not cultivated the p'o descends to earth with the *yuan shen* (original spirit) to become a ghost, which dies off relatively quickly. If, on the other hand, the Three Treasures are cultivated, then the yuan shen ascends to heaven with the h'un, thus becoming one of three stages of immortals: *Ti Hsien* (Earthly Immortal), *T'ien Hsien* (Heavenly Immortal) and *Yang Hsien* (Pure Immortal).

The reason for referring here to p'o rather than shen is that while alive the p'o benefits from the vitality and strength of ch'i, thereby increasing the life span and enhancing the health. In Taoist alchemy there is a saying, "*Replenish the Yang with Yin*". The p'o is yin, the h'un yang. Through T'ai Chi Ch'uan practices this is exactly what occurs, yang is made strong through yin.

In the T'ai Chi Ch'uan classics it says, "*From the flexible and most yielding one can become the most powerful and unyielding.*" So the use of p'o here is a symbolism for how softness and yielding can overcome the hard and unyeilding, such as water wearing away at a rock, or in Lao Tzu's analogy, "*The tongue lasts a long time because it is soft. Because they are hard, the teeth cannot outlast the tongue.*"

11. See Chapter Five, Note 2.

運氣 *Three*
Internal Breathing Methods
for Mobilizing the Ch'i

Men praise T'ai Chi Ch'uan as an internal style of boxing. They have three reasons for doing this. The first is because of the opinions of the scholarly community, which differentiates it from transcendentalism. The second reason involves its ingenious skills for restraining, grappling, seizing and obstructing attackers. These counter-offensive movements are internal and formless. Thirdly, one can employ the circulation of the internal breath.

Within the beginning procedures of T'ai Chi Ch'uan breathing, inhalation and exhalation are done through the nose and not the mouth. Ordinarily one uses the nose to inhale and the mouth to exhale, but this is not done here. Also, when reaching a high level of skill, the ch'i within the chest and stomach will become internally hot and you will be able to distinguish the stimulation of the *upper* and *lower* level breath[1]. This is called, *hsien t'ien ch'i* (before heaven breath) and *hou t'ien ch'i* (after heaven breath)[2].

When exhaling the upper level ch'i (hsien t'ien ch'i), you must exhale from the nose; then, simultaneously the lower level ch'i (hou t'ien ch'i) will return and descend into the tan-tien. When inhaling the upper level ch'i, draw it in through the nose and then, simultaneously, the lower level ch'i will return to the tan-tien to be pressed again upwards along the spine. These conditions are commonly called, "*circulating the ch'i.*"

If you simply practice the orthodox art of T'ai Chi Ch'uan the

correct levels can be attained and all the stages penetrated. Yet,
in the beginning be sure not to become excessive about training.
Avoid self-imposed obstacles to your ch'uan practice. Seek only
to practice postures in a non-aggressive manner. Inhale and
exhale naturally. The entire body should be open and relaxed,
nothing more; otherwise the body might reject or oppress the
proper maintenance of the ch'i. Guide and compel the ch'i to
sink down into the tan-tien.

It is certainly easy to be influenced onto an unorthodox path
that conflicts with this teaching. This can create problems in the
lower extremities, such as bleeding piles, hernias or other similar
afflictions.

After having attained a proper level of skill, the breath will
produce ch'i. But how to put it into use? If you do not pay
attention to the principles, the spiritual realms will not be
experienced.

The Mental Elucidation of the Thirteen Kinetic Postures says,
"*With proper breathing you can become alert and lively.*" Mind-
intent is then breathing with movement. They should be as
inextricable as the joint motion of two hands clapping together.
For if you inhale, you must exhale; and if you exhale, you must
inhale. The inhalation becomes insubstantial and the exhalation
becomes substantial (as yin becomes yang and yang becomes
yin).

Afterwards you will understand how the ch'i naturally makes the
body alert and lively; otherwise, the substantial and insubstantial
will always be indiscernible. This is how to truly examine the
errors made in practicing T'ai Chi Ch'uan because T'ai Chi
Ch'uan, in its most important aspect, is the understanding of
substantial (yang) and insubstantial (yin).

In general these teachings were conferred only on family

disciples. The teachings were divided into two sections, internal and external. The internal trains in the inhalation and exhalation of ch'i. The external trains in the boxing techniques and gestures. Generally just the bare essentials of the external methods were taught and the internal aspect was most often not transmitted. This withholding of information only disrupts and injures the proper principles of practice. It results in people being unable to comprehend naturalness and spontaneity. Possibly, in the course of time, you could intuitively comprehend its secrets. But for those who do know, to not impart their knowledge, only results in a continuing practice of not showing others.

The original books acted as a teacher to the beginner, but everyone should also have a teacher. It is impossible to acquire the teachings solely through books. This would be like food caught in the throat which must be vomited up. You need a teacher to give detailed accounts of both the method and practical use.

Generally, keep performing the circular movements of T'ai Chi Ch'uan. When the hands *push out*, you exhale; when *withdrawing* the hands, inhale. *Rising*, you inhale; *descending*, exhale. *Lifting*, you inhale; *sinking*, exhale. *Opening*, you inhale; *closing*, exhale. When moving the feet or turning the body in transition during a gesture, you perform a short breath.

Short Breath: these are short inhalations and exhalations. You still inhale and exhale, but the mental image here is of a slight stopping or restraining.

When Pushing-Hands: exhale on *Push;* exhale on *Press;* inhale on *Roll-Back* and exhale on *Ward-Off.* When being the object of Roll-Back, perform naturally a short breath; seek also a quiet mind. With a tranquil mind you can see and listen to the actions of the opponent so as not to make a serious mistake.

Being the object of Press or Push and unable to perform a
repeated inhalation, change to an exhalation, because to employ
another inhalation (to force it) advances the ch'i, dispersing it
into the four limbs. The opposite here is also true, concerning
the exhalation. In either case learn not to force the breath - do
not force an inhalation after having already inhaled; do not force
an exhalation after having already exhaled. Naturally inhale and
exhale according to circumstances.

In regards to inhaling and exhaling within the Roll-Back
posture: when first sensing the opponent's attack, exhale; with
Shoulder-Stroke, exhale; with a Push, exhale; Roll-Back, inhale.
When being the object of Shoulder-Stroke, inhale. When the
object of Roll-Back, first do a short exhalation and then inhale;
when turning the body back, seize the opportunity for Push and
even though not yet pushing, perform a short exhalation and
inhalation when the opponent steps but has not yet issued the

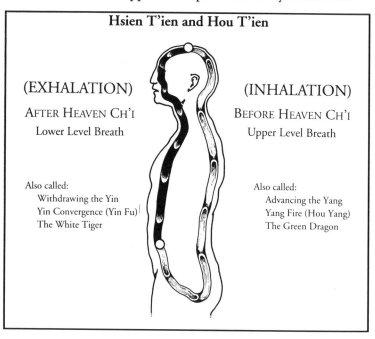

Hsien T'ien and Hou T'ien

(EXHALATION)

AFTER HEAVEN CH'I
Lower Level Breath

Also called:
    Withdrawing the Yin
    Yin Convergence (Yin Fu)
    The White Tiger

(INHALATION)

BEFORE HEAVEN CH'I
Upper Level Breath

Also called:
    Advancing the Yang
    Yang Fire (Hou Yang)
    The Green Dragon

intrinsic energy. Also, when activating the short inhalation and exhalation, watch and listen with a tranquil mind to better acquire sticky and adhering intrinsic energy.

The inhalations and exhalations for the sword, sabre, staff and san-shou, etc., along with their practical applications, are the same as with the circular forms. When the hands (or weapon) are extended, you exhale; withdrawing the hands, you must inhale; rising, you inhale; descending, you exhale; opening, you inhale; closing, you exhale. Your perception or sensations are the guide here, but do not make repeated reference to them, for every situation is different.

Ch'i Mobilization

With regard to the methods for mobilizing the internal ch'i, distinguish between the Before Heaven which mobilizes the After Heaven and the After Heaven which mobilizes the Before Heaven. These are the two types of mobilization:

1) The Before moves the After. A common saying states, "*The Before Heaven causes the After Heaven to move.*"

The ch'i in the tan-tien moves down and penetrates into the *hai ti,* then directly travels to the *wei lu* where it rises and connects with the spine to continue moving upwards, threading through the *yu chen* and *t'ien ling* points [3].

Moving downward it passes through the front of the forehead, through the center of the raphe of the upper lip, throat and down into the stomach. Reaching the navel it returns to the tan-tien, *the origin.*

2) The After moves the Before. A common saying says, "*The After Heaven mobilizes the Before Heaven.*"

The ch'i of the tan-tien moves upwards. As it does it passes through the navel, abdomen (solar plexus), throat ("adam's apple"), the raphe of the upper lip and the front of the forehead. It continues through the t'ien ling and yu chen points. It connects with the spine and moves down to the wei lu, then passes through the hai ti, moves upwards and returns to the origin - the *tan-tien*.

The above style (#2) is directly opposite to the first style. This type of ch'i mobilization, especially to the beginner, is very difficult to prove. But in the course of time you can pass beyond this condition of doubt and realize the internal ch'i. The above are the two types of circulation of the internal ch'i.

Upon completing the solo training of this kung (the exercises contained within this book) you should apply this to external use and begin training the issuance of intrinsic energy with others (pushing-hands practice). Then you will be able to correctly observe its use. If not, when needing to issue energy, you will be defeated or harmed and all your efforts will be in vain.

In terms of martial arts, the push is the highest level within T'ai Chi Ch'uan. It is not enough to just circulate the ch'i within yourself. As before, it is experience with issuing energy which enables you to defeat an opponent. Because of the internal ch'i, whether rising or descending, moving to or fro, you will be aware of the ch'i gathering in the hands. This will reveal to you how truly subtle this form of kung-fu really is. Without much basic training this will be difficult to apprehend.

Heng and Ha

There are intrinsic sounds within the inhalation and exhalation called *heng ha*.[4] Following this profound kung enables you to unite these sounds with the breath and mouth, but to be precise it is the navel (tan-tien) which works the inhalation and exhalation.

In both solo training and sparring with an opponent, the skill of heng ha is of great importance. Each one should be trained to the point of thoughtlessness, as though these words just emerge from the mouth. There are three principle reasons for training in heng ha:

The first is to use these sounds so that the internal ch'i will bring about comfort and tranquility. You can avoid being injured in an accident without having to use your martial arts skills.

The second is to use these sounds so that the intrinsic energy of the entire body will stimulate the ch'i to come out, without the slightest obstruction.

The third is to use these sounds in order to frighten the opponent. His movements will then be disorganized; his spirit and mind confused. Whether you are advancing or withdrawing, he will misinterpret you, but you will exhibit self control. Then you will be able to take advantage of his weakness and defeat him.

These two secrets of heng ha have great use. Upon learning them you will eventually employ them without being aware of it.

Heng: this has many uses at the time of either enticing or neutralizing. (*The internal ch'i is activated upon the inhalation.*)

Ha: apply at the time of seizing or issuing. (*The internal ch'i is activated upon the exhalation.*)

In the original manuscript of **The T'ai Chi Ch'uan Classic of Secret Songs**, it says:

To abide by the tan-tien is to train the internal kung, heng ha.
These two breaths are wonderful and inexhaustible.
Activity is divided; in stillness it joins; in action it follows the curve
and fully extends.
Slowness and speed should be responded to accordingly. Following
this principle you can thoroughly understand.

Also, within the inner text of the old **T'ai Chi Ch'uan Treatise**
it says:

When dealing with another (pushing-hands) and moving 'to and
fro,' sooner or later you must let loose and issue (fa) energy as if
shooting an arrow into the clouds.

How much should one nourish the ch'i? In one breath a loud sound,
Ha! is made and then withdrawn immediately (the more ch'i the
louder the sound). This is the oral transmission which was secretly
handed down. Opening this gate one can see directly into the
heavens.

From this one can understand the profound uses of these two
words, heng and ha.

CHAPTER THREE NOTES

1. **SHANG TS'ENG CH'I**: *Upper Level Ch'i* and **HSIA TS'ENG CH'I**: *Lower Level Ch'i.* Upper level ch'i represents the inhalation which is directed from the tan-tien upwards along the spine to the ni-wan, on top of the head. Lower level ch'i corresponds to the exhalation which is directed from the ni-wan through the thorax into the tan-tien along the front of the body.

Some books have suggested, erroneously, that upper and lower ch'i is a matter of directing the breath into the chest and stomach respectively. This is what the text later refers to as a "conflicting path" and "unorthodox path."

2. **HSIEN T'IEN CH'I**: *Before Heaven Breath* and **HOU T'IEN CH'I**: *After Heaven Breath.* These are the proper Taoist names for upper and lower level ch'i. Hsien t'ien ch'i is the inhalation, as it ascend upwards to heaven; hou t'ien ch'i is the exhalation as it descends downwards to earth.

3. **HAI TI**: *Sea Bottom Cavity* (coccyx)
   WEI LU: *Tail Gate Cavity* (tailbone)
   YU CHEN: *Jade Pillow Cavity* (back of the head)
   T'IEN LING: *Heavenly Spirit Cavity* (forehead)

4. **HENG HA**: Commonly translated as, *"to hum and haw."* Also means two fierce-looking spirits usually guarding a temple gate or sometimes painted on the doors.

Heng (pronounced "hun") is the sound made when being frightened. **Ha** is the sound of laughter.

When training in the solo forms or two-person exercises, the sound of heng ha is inaudible. It creates a gentle and smooth vibration internally, which benefits both the five viscera and the stimulation of ch'i. It is important to direct the sound from the tan-tien, not the throat.

In addition to the above there are three other reasons for training in heng ha:

1) Heng ha is a beginning stage of training the "*Golden Bell Kung*", wherein the ch'i protects the body against injury.

2) Master Liang states that "*Intrinsic energy is what stimulates the ch'i to be issued, otherwise the ch'i may become stagnated. Heng ha can likewise stimulate the intrinsic energy and ch'i.*"

3) If the sound is projected from the tan-tien it can be tremendously powerful and frightening to an opponent. Again, Master Liang relates this to a baby which can produce extremely loud shrieks and never suffer a sore throat because it comes from the tan-tien. Master Liang himself at 92 years old can still use this sound effectively.

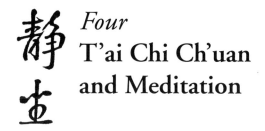

Four
T'ai Chi Ch'uan
and Meditation

People should be aware that meditation can be very beneficial. On a minor level it can nourish the body (for health); on a greater level you can enter the gate of a skilled cultivator (for immortality).

It is certain that with proper meditation practice many significant attainments will ensue; consequently, you must actively seek to acquire stillness internally. However, by no means is this stillness similar to the idea of motionlessness.[1]

The meditational aspect of T'ai Chi Ch'uan is to seek stillness within movement. Mentally they both have the same flavor; consequently, T'ai Chi Ch'uan practice has the same attainments as meditation. Both of these actively seek internal stillness. The two are identical paths.

Moreover, the rise and descent of the breath within T'ai Chi Ch'uan practice creates a complete orbit of the hsien t'ien (before heaven) ch'i, which is identical to the secret of the *golden elixir*[2] within meditation practice. This is also the very essence of T'ai Chi Ch'uan.

It is said of those who cultivate the Tao through just seated meditation: "Sitting for long periods, there is a fear that the pulses (ch'i flow) will accidently become obstructed because seated meditation can cause an excess of ch'i in the meridians." But by means of the T'ai Chi Ch'uan exercises the internal ch'i is assisted in its circulation. This is most certainly not an empty or false statement. An old, often stated Taoist verse says, "To cultivate the Tao without first cultivating the body is useless."

Internal cultivation is called, *the highest level of cultivation.* The levels in full are: the highest level termed *great accomplishment* the lowest level called *small accomplishment* and the middle level of *accomplishment.* These levels have three divisions, but in the end they are one in the same.

Civil and Martial Cultivation

Civil cultivation is internal and martial cultivation is external. The internal, physical culture is the disciplining of the ching, ch'i and shen. Martial matters (practicing the boxing arts) are the external culture. Cultivating both of these, you can completely unite the internal and external aspects, the inside and outside, figuratively. This is the highest level of achievement.

The lowest level is to know the civil, physical culture and attainments or the martial matters and attainments on a solely intellectual basis.

Meditation and civil cultivation are one; therefore, meditation and T'ai Chi Ch'uan share a very close relationship. An ode says, "*Contemplate without disturbance.*" Kung-fu Tzu[3] said, "*Stillness is benevolence.*" Meng Tzu[4] said, "*Just do not move the mind.*" All of these verses on stillness are extremely important. When you can sit in stillness, the mind will become level and the ch'i will circulate harmoniously. The mind-intent will cause the body to remain upright, and all your thoughts will be clear and tranquil. Then at the time of pushing-hands, it will not matter what energy is employed (there are numerous *chings*)[5], as it will not be coming from a confused mind.

The method for stilling the mind consists primarily of controlling your temper. Control means to harness your courage which is internal (not arrogance which is external). With robust courage the ch'i will be strengthened. If the courage is not robust, then the spirit (shen) will be weak.

So at the time of performing the meditation exercises you can become very confused. Not only might you not progress but you may harm yourself. If possible you should follow the orthodox practice (the teachings handed down from founder to master, to student etc.). Following this is just as important with respect to T'ai Chi Ch'uan practice. This will prevent the spreading of corrupt practices.

Sitting Practice

The correct manner for sitting is either the half lotus (one leg crossed with the foot placed on the opposite thigh), full lotus (both legs crossed and placed on opposite thighs) or the common seated posture (with legs crossed but not placed on the thighs). All of these will do.

It is necessary to suspend the head to keep the body upright (retain a light and sensitive energy on top of the head), sink the shoulders and hollow the chest. Relax and open the entire body. Place the tongue up against the roof of the mouth. The lips and teeth join lightly together. Slightly close both eyes. This is called, "letting down the screens." With respect to the two hands - place the back of the left palm in the center of the right palm close to the front of the lower abdomen (tan-

Full Lotus Posture

tien), lightly and loosely above the thighs.

Half Lotus Posture

Afterwards, when the mind and thoughts are settled and the navel region is relaxed, when there is no "I" or "others", and all confused thinking is utterly ignored, then you can bring an end to the constant examining and turn back the hearing (employ internal listening, rather than external). In a common Taoist saying it is stated, *"Be ever cautious to put a stop to the Five Thieves (joy, anger, pleasure, grief and lust)."* [6]

Pay heed to the ears and the result will be ears that do not listen externally; then the sperm (*ching*) can be restored in the kidneys (*sheng*).

Pay heed to the eyes and the result will be eyes that do not gaze

Cross-legged Posture

externally; then the spirit (h'un, *heavenly bound spirit*) can be restored in the liver (*kan*).

Pay heed to the mouth and the result will be tacit understanding without speech; then the spirit (*shen*) can be restored in the heart (*hsin*).

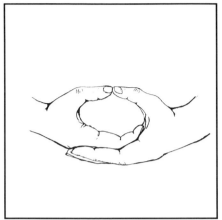

Hand Position (A)
Comment: When using either hand position A or B it is immaterial whether the left hand supports the right hand or vice versa

Pay heed to the nose and the result will be a nose that does not smell externally; then the spirit (p'o, *earthly bound spirit*) can be restored in the lungs (*fei*).

Pay heed to the mind and then, when the "mind-intent" is applied, it will be without limit (*wu-chi*); then the mind (*i*) can be restored to the spleen (*p'i*).

Ching (*regenerative energy*); shen (*human spirit*); h'un (*heavenly spirit*); p'o (*earthly spirit*); i (*mind-intent*); hsin (*heart*); kan (*liver*); fei (*lungs*); p'i (*spleen*) and sheng (*kidneys*) - each will undergo restoration; each will return to their natural state. This results in a natural manifestation of the zenith[7], where yet another state of perception arises.

The time periods for meditation should be once in the morning after waking and once before bedtime. In the event that you have some spare time in the afternoon, you should meditate once here also. It does not matter whether the periods are long or short; for example, one quarter of an hour, one half hour

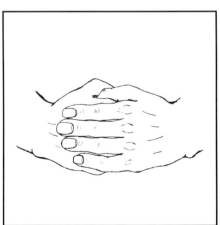

Hand Position (B)

or even one full hour; any of these will suffice.

With sitting you can attain delightful states. The entire body, internally and externally, will be exceptionally comfortable and pleasing. Within the mouth, the tongue is depressed (up against the palate). This will cause the saliva to gush forth which will taste sweet and pleasant when swallowed[8]. This is called, "the completion of fire and water [9]." This is the unification of the mercury (elixir) or *ch'ien* (heaven) and *k'un* (earth). [10]

When beginning to learn seated meditation, the four limbs will become agitated and uncomfortable. Thoughts will be wild and it will be difficult to stop the thinking process. Even after a long time they will stop and then go; but naturally, over a course of time, you will be able to get rid of them.

T'ai Chi double fish symbol in conjunction with the Eight Diagram arrangement created by Fu Hsi

When beginning to learn, it is absolutely necessary to pay attention to one's inability to activate the ch'i. Breath only through the nose; seek to master this naturally. To activate the ch'i it is necessary to achieve this through proper regulation. Then and only then, can you train the ch'i; otherwise, it will be easy to form a corrupt practice in

which the mind-intent causes the ch'i to rise upwards, resulting
in congestion in the brain. Eventually you will suffer from a
disorder in the nervous system. The spirit will be divided
internally, causing suffering from the heart and stomach
ailments. If the spirit should fall, then you may suffer from
bleeding piles, bowels or a ruptured hernia.

The benefits of seated meditation follow after a long period of
practice. When everything unites at the aperture and navel, then
the ch'i can be circulated. This is great accomplishment kung-fu,
but you cannot accomplish it without the true orthodox
teaching.

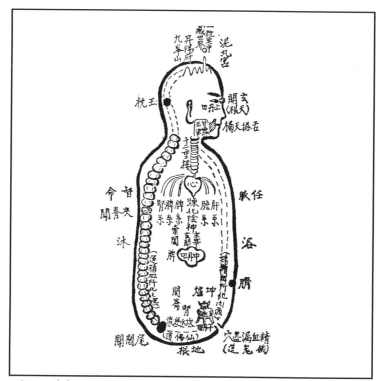

*Original diagram of the Hsien T'ien and Hou T'ien circut, according to
the Taoist sect Lung Men* (Dragon Door).

Mobilizing The Ch'i

These are the proper methods for mobilizing the ch'i. A concise description is as follows:

ONE:

Within T'ai Chi Ch'uan, the after heaven (ch'i) is distinct from the before heaven (ch'i). They are, however, alike; just the direction of circulation is different.

From the *tan-tien*, the ch'i passes through the *hai ti*, directly to the *wei lu* and then upwards along the spine. It then passes through the *yu chen* and flows along the forehead (t'ien ling). Moving downwards along the front of the forehead to the raphe of the upper lip, it flows through the "adam's apple" into the pit of the stomach, and then into the navel, thus returning to the *tan-tien*.

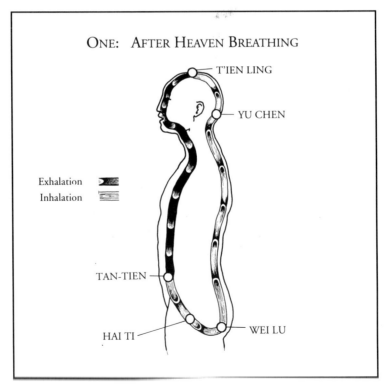

ONE: AFTER HEAVEN BREATHING

T'IEN LING

YU CHEN

Exhalation
Inhalation

TAN-TIEN

HAI TI

WEI LU

TWO:

From the *shan ken* [11] the ch'i moves upwards to the *t'ien ling*.
Pressing on in reverse motion, the ch'i moves down, passing
through the *yu chen* and down along the spine until reaching the
wei lu. It rises up through the intestinal region, returns to
connect with the back of the spine and moves upwards. Passing
beyond the *yu chen* and *t'ien ling* it again moves down along the
front through the *shan ken* and the *ch'eng chiang* [12] point.
Swallow the saliva[13]. The ch'i then returns to the *tan-tien*.

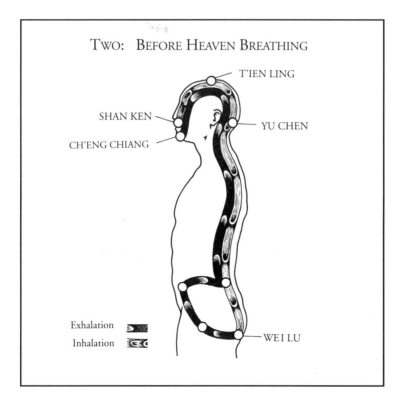

TWO: BEFORE HEAVEN BREATHING

T'IEN LING

SHAN KEN

YU CHEN

CH'ENG CHIANG

Exhalation
Inhalation

WEI LU

THREE:

Small Heavenly Circuits[14]

A. Upper tan-tien or *hsuan kuan* [15]: between the two eyes and
slightly upwards about three centimeters.
Yu chu [16]: at the tip of the nose.
Chung lou [17]: by the great, protruding hollow and down one and
one half inches.

B. Middle tan-tien or *shan chung* [18]: between the bones which
resemble the character for man (人 , *jen*).
Ling t'ai [19]: at the navel and up one and one half inches.
Tu fu [20]: eight centimeters up from the navel.

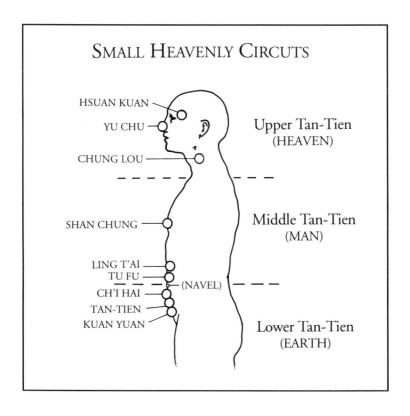

SMALL HEAVENLY CIRCUTS

HSUAN KUAN
YU CHU

CHUNG LOU

Upper Tan-Tien
(HEAVEN)

SHAN CHUNG

Middle Tan-Tien
(MAN)

LING T'AI
TU FU
CH'I HAI — (NAVEL)
TAN-TIEN
KUAN YUAN

Lower Tan-Tien
(EARTH)

C. Lower tan-tien or *ch'i hai* [21]: Down one inch.
Tan-tien: down two inches from the navel.
Kuan yuan [22]: down three inches from the navel.

Each of these three openings in each circuit should be visualized as having a three inch diameter [23.]

FOUR:

Greater Heavenly Circuit

1. *From Wu Chi* (*yin tang:* the space between the two eyebrows) and the *T'ai Chi* (at the angle of the sun and moon).

2. *Embrace the Sun and Moon* (at a direct angle from the sun and moon) upwards to *Mt. Kunlun* (the topmost point on top of the center of the head).

3. *Ride a Black Ox Through the Dark Valley Pass* (in the neck, behind the two, soft, fleshy areas — the center of the two sides of this point).

4. *Directly Arrive At Heaven's Heart* (on the spine there are joints one, two and three which protrude. The points are within these empty caverns).

5. *Small Rest at the Central Mt. Hsu Mi* (above on both sides of the waist).

6. *Seeing a Dragon at the Bottom of the Sea* (yin in front , yin behind - the soft, fleshy space between).

7. *In the Field* (to both *yung chuan* points by moving downwards on the back of the legs).

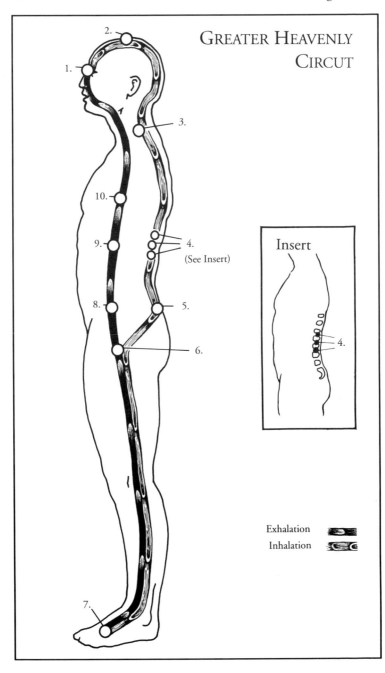

GREATER HEAVENLY
CIRCUT

Insert

4.
(See Insert)

Insert

4.

Exhalation
Inhalation

8. *Plant the Jade, Rest and Plough* (behind the navel, seven centimeters; in front of spine three centimeters. Return through the back of the legs, stopping to rest with an inhalation and exhalation).

9. *Ten-Thousand Images* (between the two openings).

10. *Returning to Spring* (below the *chung lou,* one and one half inches; above one and one-half inches of the *shan chung* - within the upper front of the middle of the chest).

Concluding Comment:

The ch'i within men's bodies is like a fiery sphere. It will also do to follow the reverse revolutions of ch'i circuits. Ultimately, both circuits are natural.

In regards to seated meditation and fixed concentration, the motive is enlightenment; good roots will appear and culminate in great accomplishments. In every man exists this nature (of enlightenment and good roots). Therefore, in the practice of T'ai Chi Ch'uan and in seeking to attain the skills inherent to it, compose a plan to cultivate the mind and body simultaneously; otherwise, the training of seated meditation *kung-fu*[24] will accomplish little.

It is essential to know that the Tao of sitting takes many years, as it does with learning and practicing T'ai Chi Ch'uan. Seated *kung*[25] acts as an aid, but it is insufficient in itself for acquiring the skills of T'ai Chi Ch'uan.

How much training does it take to accomplish all this? If you take the door of short cuts there will be no progress. It is as if measuring nine mountains. "To fail in completion by one basketful," (almost successful). How unfortunate!

CHAPTER FOUR NOTES

1. Stillness is ultimately a state of mind, whether one is performing the movements of T'ai Chi Ch'uan or seated in meditation. Stillness is internal, whereas motionlessness is external. Stillness of the mind means that the mind (rational thinking) is emptied, while the mind-intent is then functional, there is heightened perception, inner awareness, etc.

2. **CHIN TAN:** *Golden Elixir.* Internal alchemy also calls this "the pill of immortality," which is produced by disciplining and refining the Three Treasures (ching, ch'i and shen).

3. **KUNG-FU TZU:** *Confucius* 551-479 B.C. China's greatest sage and most influential philosopher. His teachings became one of China's three great teachings, which are Confucianism, Taoism and Buddhism. *Jen che ching* means that only through internal stillness can one truly be kind, loving and humane, because a still mind has no greed or selfishness.

4. **MENG TZU:** *Mencius* Born 372 B.C. An ardent supporter of Confucianism. His writing, **The Book of Mencius** forms the fourth Book of the Confucian classics, (The Four Books). *Pu tung hsin* literally means "do not make use of the rational thinking mind (hsin)."

5. **CHING:** (pronounced *chin*) *Intrinsic Energies.* The Yang family of T'ai Chi Ch'uan records that there are twenty-five major chin and numerous minor ones which are developed in the successful practice of T'ai Chi Ch'uan.

6. This paragraph is pointing out the benefits of stillness in relation to the Five Activities (*Wu-Hsing*: Metal, Fire, Wood, Water and Earth), which permeate Taoist philosophy, indeed all Chinese thought. Some have erroneously translated Wu-Hsing as "*Five Elements,*" however the underlying idea here is not material substance, rather the *activity* of the element. There is no space here to go into great detail on Wu-Hsing theory, however in light of this material the gist of the teaching is as follows:

The Five Thieves (*Wu-Tse*) negatively effect the Five Viscera (*Wu-*

Tsang). However, through stillness and internal cultivation these Five Viscera can be positively affected by the Five Spiritual Energies. The following chart is given below to elucidate further.

Five Thieves	Five Viscera	Five Spiritual Energies
Joy	Heart	*Shen* (Spirit)
Anger	Liver	*H'un* (Heavenly Spirit)
Pleasure	Lungs	*P'o* (Earthly Spirit)
Grief	Spleen*(or stomach)	*I* (Mind-Intent)*(or *ch'i*)
Lust	Kidneys	*Ching* (Regenerative)

*The spleen and mind-intent are identical to stomach and ch'i respectively. It is a matter of discretion as to the terminology.

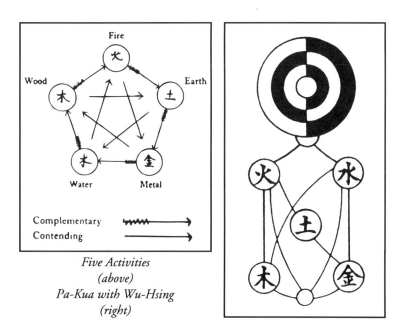

Five Activities
(above)
Pa-Kua with Wu-Hsing
(right)

7. **T'IEN HSIN:** Literally, "a mind in the heavens," a boundless and limitless state of mind, therefore "zenith".

8. Unlike Western notions of saliva being a negative substance, the Taoists and Buddhists view it as a valuable substance for health and spiritual cultivation, calling it "Divine Water".

9. The ch'i (heat in stomach) uniting with the saliva which is gulped down into the tan-tien. In Taoist alchemy ingesting saliva and breath are two important practices. Also, see Note 5, Chapter 2.

10. **CH'IEN:** *The Creative;* **K'UN:** *The Receptive,* from the *I-Ching* (Classic on Changes). Ch'ien represents yang in its highest aspect; K'un represents yin in its highest aspect.

11. **SHAN KEN:** *Base of the Mountain.*

12. **CH'ENG CHIANG:** *Fluid Container.*

13. **YEN HSIEN:** *Swallow the Saliva.*

14. **HSAIO CHOU T'IEN:** *Small Heavenly Circuit or Microcosmic Orbit.*

15. **SHANG TAN-TIEN:** *Upper Tan-Tien.*
    HSUAN KUAN: *Mysterious or Dark Pass.*

16. **YU CHU:** *Jade Pillar* (the nose).

17. **CHUNG LOU:** *Big Tower.*

18. **CHUNG TAN-TIEN:** *Middle Tan-Tien.*
    SHAN CHUNG: *Inner Deer.*

19. **LING T'AI:** *Spiritual Terrace.*

20. **TU FU:** *Earthen Caldron.*

21. **HSIA TAN-TIEN:** *Lower Tan-Tien.*
    CH'I HAI: *Ocean of Ch'i.*

22. **KUAN YUAN:** *Original Pass.*

23 The visualization of A, B and C or Small Heavenly Circuit are three separated practices. (See attached illustrations.) They are to be performed successively from Upper, Middle to Lower, with the circuits performed in a clockwise manner.

24. **KUNG-FU:** *Fu* in this term adds to the meaning of *kung* the idea of a sage, master or hero.

25. **KUNG:** meritorious effort; efficacious practice.

Five
T'ai Chi Ch'i-Kung

**Fundamental Procedures for Strengthening
and Mobilizing the Ch'i**

The vital importance of the ch'i within man's body was
explained in the earlier sections, **"A Discourse on Mind-Intent
and Ch'i"** and **"Internal Ch'i Breathing Methods for
Mobilizing the Ch'i."** However, the actual training procedures
for these are not explained within the two earlier discourses.
Here is a simplified and elementary procedure.

The extinction of Ch'i results in our death; consequently, we
should fear losing it, as it is not easily accumulated. The ancient
books sought to explain these particulars in full detail, but
lacked clarity.

To perform the exercises for strengthening and mobilizing the
ch'i, the following principles must be applied:

The breath must be in unison with the movements of the body,
doing so with the rise and descent of either the hsien t'ien ch'i
(before heaven ch'i) or the hou t'ien ch'i (after heaven ch'i),
which are respectively, related to upper level breathing and lower

level breathing. Learning and practicing this enables you to
directly follow in the footsteps of the ancient masters and to
enter within the inner chambers of these methods.

More than anything else, avoid being unwittingly sidetracked;
otherwise, all your efforts will be in vain. This procedure for
strengthening and mobilizing the ch'i must be gradually trained
and developed through regular practice if the internal ch'i is to
be stimulated so as to be exhibited externally, as is the case with
T'ai Chi Ch'uan. When your environment does not permit you
to practice T'ai Chi Ch'uan (there is no room in which to
practice the circular movements and stepping actions) you may
utilize this exercise.

T'ai Chi Ch'i-Kung allows the sinews and bones to be stretched
and expanded, causing the blood and ch'i to unite, increasing
the internal energy. Half-measures are not enough. You need to
train hard in order to cultivate the ch'i.

In my observation of the students and disciples of previous
generations of the Yang family, many were well acquainted with
this particular exercise of T'ai Chi Ch'i-Kung, but few had
access to its secrets. The reason for this was that the family
instructors were unwilling and unconcerned about teaching
others (non-family members). They trusted only themselves.
How pitiful!

Some people may be inclined to treat this exercise as just another
form of *Pa Tuan Chin* [1] or deep breathing. Such exercises will, of
course, produce some benefit, but far less than what can be
achieved by T'ai Chi Ch'i-Kung. Strive to learn this method
well; it should not be treated lightly.

Comment:

When performing deep breathing to produce ch'i, you must seek to do it as naturally as possible. Whether inhaling or exhaling, it must be performed slowly and gradually. Each breath should be taken slowly and without restraint; it should not be repressed by being too regulatory which produces negative circulation. It is expected that you will train carefully.

T'ai Chi Ch'i-Kung Exercise

The following pages describe and illustrate the twenty-one gestures of the T'ai Chi Ch'i-Kung exercise.

FIRST GESTURE:

Place both feet in line with one another in a fixed stance, with the head held erect. Retain a light and sensitive energy on top of the head. The eyes gaze levelly to the front. Hold the tongue against the roof of the mouth and lightly close the lips and teeth. This is the same stance as taken with the T'ai Chi Ch'uan Beginning Posture. Exhale through the nose. The internal heat produced by the breath is divided into two stages, upper and lower.

First, inhale through the nose and then, sinking the ch'i gradually to the tan-tien, exhale. Lower the shoulders and elbows. Hollow the chest and raise the back. Press the palms of both hands downwards; extend the fingertips to the front, but do not use muscular force. Slightly bend the arms and elbows. Relax the whole body. Raise the spirit of vitality; suspend the head from above as if by a string.

Comment:

In order to begin learning this gesture you must first breathe through the nose so that the ch'i can enter the hands. The ch'i should be made to rise and descend, but follow a natural course.

This gesture is one movement. The internal ch'i is inhaled and exhaled in an alternate manner in one circuit[2]. There is a pause at the completion of the exhalation.

- *ends with an exhalation; one circuit*
- *retain a light and sensitive energy on top of the head*
- *when exhaling, sink the ch'i to the tan-tien*

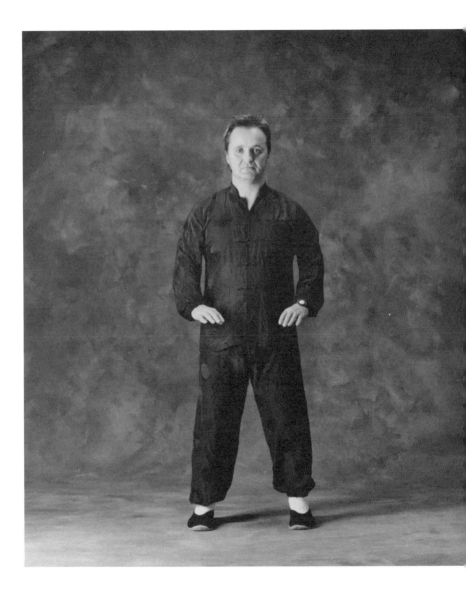

First Gesture

SECOND GESTURE:

Both hands simultaneously move upwards to the left and right sides. The arms stop upon reaching shoulder level. The palms face downward; the fingertips extend outwards. The ch'i gathers in, as the two hands open and separate and the inhalation enters through the nose. Direct the ch'i from the tan-tien upwards allowing it to adhere to the back of the spine. After the two hands are openly divided on line with one another, the movement momentarily stops. Alternate the inhalation to an exhalation. Sink the lower level breath into the tan-tien.

Comment:

This gesture has one pause within the movement and internally the ch'i makes one circuit.

- *one inhalation, one exhalation*
- *when inhaling, adhere the ch'i to the spine*
- *when exhaling, sink the ch'i to the tan-tien*
- *both arms extend outward at shoulder level*

Second Gesture

THIRD GESTURE:

Both hands simultaneously move inwards towards the front and
join. Inhale the upper level breath through the nose and adhere
the ch'i to the spine. Then perform lower level breathing and
sink the ch'i to the tan-tien.

Third Gesture, Part One

Place the right hand on top of the left, to form a criss-cross
shape with the palms facing down. Hollow the chest and raise
the back. The two hands simultaneously turn downward with
the palms facing towards the body. The fingertips hang
downward. Inhale the upper level breath; exhale the lower level
breath and sink the ch'i to the tan-tien. This gesture has two
circuits of the ch'i, two inhalations and two exhalations.

• *two inhalations, two exhalations*
• *when inhaling, adhere the ch'i to the spine*
• *when exhaling, sink the ch'i to the tan-tien*

Third Gesture, Part Two

FOURTH GESTURE:

Turn both hands inwards and over in a circular manner, circling
the right hand until it is inside between the body and the left
hand. Both palms now face the body. During the hand
movement, bend both knees so that the body lowers into a slight
squatting position. Inhale, operating the upper level breath, and
adhere the ch'i to the spine. This gesture activates the internal
ch'i in one circuit.

• *one inhalation, one exhalation*
• *when inhaling, adhere the ch'i to the spine*

Fourth Gesture

FIFTH GESTURE:

Both hands simultaneously turn upward but move downward
and stop when they are beside the pelvis. Extend the fingertips
to the front. During the hand movement raise the body upward
by straightening your knees. Inhale the upper level breath and
adhere the ch'i to the spine. Exhale the lower level breath and
sink the ch'i to the tan-tien. There is no pause between Gesture
Four and Five so that the ch'i makes one more circuit.

* *one inhalation, one exhalation*
* *when inhaling, adhere the ch'i to the spine*
* *when exhaling, sink the ch'i to the tan-tien*

Fifth Gesture

SIXTH GESTURE:

With the palms still facing upwards, move them forward, out
and upward until both extend at the level of the chest. The
palms face upward and the fingertips extend to the front. At the
same time, bend both knees slowly, moving the body into a
slight squatting position. Inhale, activating the upper level
breath and sink the ch'i to the tan-tien. This gesture has one
circuit of the internal ch'i.

• *one inhalation, one exhalation*
• *when exhaling, sink the ch'i to the tan-tien*

Sixth Gesture

SEVENTH GESTURE:

Separate both hands and move them to the left and right side so
that they are in line with the shoulders. The palms face upwards
and the fingertips stretch outwards. As both hands open and
separate, inhale to work the ch'i, adhering it to the spine.

After the hands open and separate, halt the movement
momentarily. At this point exhale and gradually raise the body
upwards by slowly straightening the knees. During the
exhalation sink the ch'i to the tan-tien. This gesture is one
movement and completes one circuit of the internal ch'i.

* *one inhalation, one exhalation*
* *both arms extend outwards at shoulder level*
* *when inhaling, adhere the ch'i to the spine*

Seventh Gesture

EIGHTH GESTURE:

Turn both hands upwards and inwards, gradually forming them into fists as you do so. During this motion, move the fists upward until they reach the sides of the ears, with the "tiger mouths" facing upward. Do not clench the fists too tightly. Very little energy should be utilized when raising the arms (no tension). Relax and open the whole body; hollow the chest and raise the back. Simultaneously bend the legs and lower the body into a squatting position. Inhale to activate the upper level breath and adhere the ch'i along the spine. Exhale to activate the lower level breath and sink the ch'i to the tan-tien. This gesture has one circuit of the internal ch'i.

• *one inhalation, one exhalation*
• *when inhaling, adhere the ch'i to the spine*

Eighth Gesture

NINTH GESTURE:

Both hands simultaneously turn over and out, so that the "tiger mouths" face one another with the palms of the hands (in fist position) facing outward. Inhale to activate the upper level breath and exhale to sink the ch'i to the tan-tien. Along with the eighth gesture, the internal ch'i is strung together in one action, therefore, there is no pause in the movement. This gesture has one circuit of the internal ch'i.

• *one inhalation, one exhalation*
• *when inhaling, adhere the ch'i to the spine*
• *when exhaling, sink the ch'i to the tan-tien*

Ninth Gesture

TENTH GESTURE:

Both fists change into open palms, while simultaneously moving
to the left and right sides as the arms extend. The forearms move
downward as the hands are opening. By the time the forearms
are level with the shoulders (left arm off the left shoulder and
right arm off the right shoulder) the palms face downward. The
fingers stretch outward. Straighten the knees to slowly raise the
body. Inhale to activate the upper level breath and cause the ch'i
to rise upwards along the spine. Exhale to sink the ch'i to the
tan-tien. This gesture has one circuit of the internal ch'i.

• *one inhalation, one exhalation*
• *when exhaling, sink the ch'i into the tan-tien*

Tenth Gesture

ELEVENTH GESTURE:

Both palms gradually return to a fist position.

1. Move the hands inwards and upwards and position them
beside the ears with the "tiger mouths" facing upward. Hollow
the chest and raise the back. The knees bend to lower the body
into a slight squatting position. This is just like the eighth
posture. Inhale to activate the upper level breath; exhale to
activate the lower level breath and sink the ch'i to the tan-tien.

Eleventh Gesture, Part One

2. Both fists simultaneously rise until they are beside the temples. The knees slowly straighten to raise the body gradually upwards. Inhale to activate the upper level breath, adhering the ch'i to the spine.

3. The two fists continue to rise upwards until they are above the head. Exhale to activate the lower level breath and sink the ch'i to the tan-tien.

This gesture has three actions, with two circuits of the internal ch'i.

* *two inhalations, two exhalations*
* *when inhaling adhere the ch'i to the spine*

Eleventh Gesture, Part Two

TWELFTH GESTURE:

Both fists change into open palms.

1. Push both hands simultaneously upwards as though to support something weighted, with the palms facing upwards and the fingers of each hand pointing to those of the other. Raise the body slightly upwards by straightening the knees and raising the heels off the ground. Inhale to activate the upper level breath.

Twelfth Gesture, Part One

2. Turn both hands inwards so that they cross at the wrists. This cross-like position has the right hand on top and the left underneath with each palm facing outwards. Exhale the lower level breath so that the ch'i sinks to the tan-tien.

Twelfth Gesture, Part Two

3. Lower both hands simultaneously until they are beside the pelvic area, with the palms facing upwards and the fingers pointing to the front. Lower the heels gradually.

Twelfth Gesture, Part Three

The original position is now restored, as in the fifth gesture. Inhale to activate the upper level breath and exhale to sink the ch'i to the tan-tien.

This gesture has three movements and two circuits of the internal ch'i.

- *two inhalations, two exhalations*
- *when exhaling, the ch'i sinks to the tan-tien*
- *when inhaling, the ch'i adheres to the spine*

Twelfth Gesture, Part Four

THIRTEENTH GESTURE:

1. Hold the head erect. Turn both hands simultaneously inwards so that they join in front of the lower abdomen. The palms face upwards and the thumbs of each hand face one another. The left hand is above the right. Inhale so that the ch'i adheres to the back, along the spine, and exhale to sink the ch'i to the tan-tien.

Thirteenth Gesture, Part One

2. Both hands remain where they are. The head follows the waist
and the torso in a leftward rotating gesture. The gaze remains
level as the head turns toward the back. Pause when the neck is
unable to turn any further. Inhale to activate the upper level
breath and exhale to activate the lower level breath.

Thirteenth Gesture, Part Two

3. The head and waist return to the original position facing the front. Inhale and exhale to activate the upper and lower level breaths respectively.

4. The head follows the waist by making a rightward rotating gesture. As the head turns, the gaze remains level. The head stops when it is unable to turn any further. The breath pattern is the same as described above.

5. The head and waist return to the original position facing the front. Repeat the same breath pattern as above.

This gesture has five circuits of the internal ch'i.

Comment:

As discussed, this gesture involves the turning of the head to the left and right sides with a level gaze. You can augment these movements with two or three more rotations; however, this is optional. When turning, keep the head upright and straight, especially when pausing at the completion of a turn.

- *five inhalations, five exhalations*
- *when exhaling, the ch'i sinks into the tan-tien*
- *when inhaling, the ch'i adheres to the spine*

Thirteenth Gesture, Part Three

FOURTEENTH GESTURE:

Turn both palms inwards, over and down so that the back of the
hands face upwards. Bend the upper part of the body over to the
front into a low, stooping position. Place both palms upon the
ground and hold the fingers of each hand opposite one another.
The knees remain straight but not locked throughout the entire
movement.

When first practicing this gesture, in the event that the hands
are unable to be placed upon the ground, it will be quite
adequate to stop and rest at a comfortable point, as this pressing
gesture must not be forced. In the course of time the waist will
become more pliable and you will be able to naturally touch the
ground. Exhale as you bend over to activate the lower level
breath and sink the ch'i to the tan-tien.

The movements of this gesture circuit the ch'i once. This gesture
(the bending over) must flow immediately after Gesture
Thirteen so that the same exhalation can be maintained for
both.

Comment:

The movements of this gesture involve bending at the waist and
rising up again. They can be augmented with either two or three
more of such actions.

• *one exhalation, one inhalation*
• *the exhalation occurs during the bending with the ch'i sinking into
the tan-tien*
• *the inhalation occurs if you perform several movements. The rise
involves an inhalation and is connected with the first part of the
fifteenth gesture.*

Fourteenth Gesture

FIFTEENTH GESTURE:

Raise the upper body to an upright position. Cross both hands
so that the palms face inwards. The right hand is on the outside
and the left on the inside. Hollow the chest and raise the back.
Now move the body down into a slight squatting position by
gradually bending the knees. Inhale as you raise your upper body
to an erect position, and exhale during the squatting motion.

* *one inhalation, one exhalation*
* *when inhaling, the ch'i adheres to the spine*

Fifteenth Gesture

SIXTEENTH GESTURE:

1. Move the left hand upwards as if you were lifting something with the palm facing upwards. Simultaneously press the right hand downward. The right palm faces down and the fingers extend to the front. Raise the body gradually upwards as your knees straighten. The upper level breath is stimulated when inhaling; exhaling enables the ch'i to sink to the tan-tien.

2. Move the left hand downwards and the right hand upward at the same time and join them in the criss-cross position in front of the chest. Now the left hand is on the outside and the right hand on the inside. Hollow the chest and raise the back as your body slowly sinks into a squatting position with both knees bending. Inhale to activate the upper level breath and adhere the ch'i to the spine. Exhale to sink the ch'i to the tan-tien.

This gesture involves two inhalations and two exhalations with two circuits of the internal ch'i.

- *two inhalations, two exhalations*
- *when exhaling, the ch'i sinks to the tan-tien*
- *when inhaling, the ch'i adheres to the spine*

Sixteenth Gesture

SEVENTEENTH GESTURE:

1. Move the right hand upwards as if you were lifting something
with the palm facing upwards. Press the left palm down at the
same time and extend the fingers to the front. Raise the body
gradually upwards as your knees slowly straighten. Inhale to
activate the upper level breath and adhere the ch'i to the spine.
Exhale to sink the ch'i to the tan-tien.

2. Move both hands to the front of the chest and join them in a
criss-cross position. This is just like the fifteenth gesture. Hollow
the chest and raise the back. The body slowly sinks into a slight
squatting position as you bend both knees. Inhale to activate the
upper level breath and adhere the ch'i to the spine; exhale to
activate the lower level breath and sink the ch'i to the tan-tien.

This gesture has two inhalations and two exhalations with two
circuits of the ch'i.

* *two inhalations, two exhalations*
* *when exhaling, the ch'i sinks into the tan-tien*
* *when inhaling, the ch'i adheres to the spine*

Seventeenth Gesture

EIGHTEENTH GESTURE:

Turn both hands so that the palms face inwards and the fingers hang downwards. Raise the body by straightening the knees. Inhale to activate the upper level breath and exhale to sink the ch'i to the tan-tien.

This gesture has one circuit of the internal ch'i.

- *one inhalation, one exhalation*
- *when inhaling, adhere the ch'i to the spine*
- *when exhaling, sink the ch'i to the tan-tien*

Eighteenth Gesture

NINETEENTH GESTURE:

Turn both hands so that they circle inward, upward and over. The right hand turns until it is closest to the body. Both palms now face inwards. The knees bend to lower the body into a squatting position. Inhale to adhere the ch'i to the spine and exhale to sink the ch'i to the tan-tien.

This gesture has one circuit of the internal ch'i; it is the same as that of Gesture Four.

* *one inhalation, one exhalation*
* *when inhaling, the ch'i adheres to the spine*

Nineteenth Gesture

TWENTIETH GESTURE:

Move both hands downwards towards the rear and position
them beside the pelvic area. The palms face upwards and the
fingers extend to the front. Gradually raise the body upwards, by
straightening the knees slightly. Inhale to activate the upper level
breath and exhale to sink the ch'i to the tan-tien.

This gesture has both an inhalation and an exhalation, with one
circuit of the internal ch'i. It involves the same movement as
Gesture Five; therefore, there is no pause between this and the
previous gesture.

- *one inhalation, one exhalation*
- *when inhaling, adhere the ch'i to the spine*

Twentieth Gesture

TWENTY-FIRST GESTURE:

Raise both hands upwards to the left and right sides respectively until they are beside the rib area. Turn the palms down and lower them while your body rises as the knees straighten. This returns you to the original position of Gesture One.

This gesture flows directly after the last one, so that the exhalation is maintained from one to the other. When exhaling, sink the ch'i to the tan-tien.

- *when exhaling, sink the ch'i to the tan-tien*
- *suspend the top of the head with a light and sensitive energy*
- *lower the shoulders and hang the elbows*
- *relax the entire body*

After completing the entire set of these gestures, stop and rest for a short period; then walk about to circulate the ch'i and blood. Return to the original position and rest.

Twenty-First Gesture

Original Illustrations

Note: *Mr. Chen comments at the end of the book that the drawings within the text may be incorrect. In the case of the T'ai Chi Ch'i-Kung exercise drawings, the feet should be separated at shoulder-width so that the ch'i can flow freely through the buttocks and coccyx region.*

— Translator

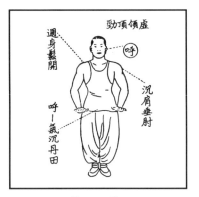

Gesture One

Gesture Two   *Gesture Three*

T'ai Chi Ch'i-Kung

Gesture Four   Gesture Five

Gesture Six   Gesture Seven

Gesture Eight   Gesture Nine

Gesture Ten   Gesture Eleven

Gesture Twelve   Gesture Thirteen

Gesture Fourteen   Gesture Fifteen

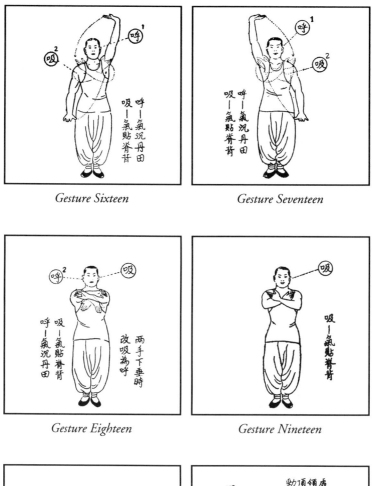

Gesture Sixteen

Gesture Seventeen

Gesture Eighteen

Gesture Nineteen

Gesture Twenty

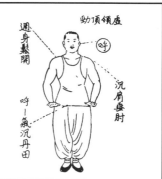

Gesture Twenty-One

Chapter Five Notes

1. **PA TUAN CHIN:** *Eight Pieces of Brocade.* A very ancient form of
Tao Yin (Taoist breathing exercises) attributed to Chung Li-ch'uan
(also known as Han Chung-li) of the Han Dynasty. Chung Li-ch'uan
was the teacher of Lu Tung-pin, one of the Eight Immortals and
founder of the Complete Reality Sect.

The exercises of Pa Tuan Chin have been also attributed to Chen
Tuan, the teacher of the famous Taoist immortal, Chang San-feng,
who is credited with inventing T'ai Chi Ch'uan.

Pa Tuan Chin has both seated and standing exercises, in both hard and
soft styles. The seated exercises are extremely effective. However, in my
opinion, the standing form is not as effective as the T'ai Chi Ch'i-
Kung exercise explained in this book.

2. *Circuit* will throughout mean not only one complete cycle of
inhalation and exhalation, but as well a visualization of ch'i ascending
up the spine to the top of the head, and descending down the front of
the body into the tan-tien.

Six
Training Exercises

1. EXTENDING THE CH'I[1]

After practicing the entire set of T'ai Chi Ch'i-Kung exercises (or the circular form of T'ai Chi Ch'uan, Tui-Shou, Ta-Lu, etc.) perform this supplemental exercise.

Preparation:

Separate both feet so that they are parallel to each other with the distance being slightly broader than the width of the shoulders. Drop the body into a horse stance, a low squatting position with the knees well bent.

Extending the Ch'i, to the front.

The upper body must be upright and erect. Retain a light and sensitive energy on top of the head. Relax the waist and buttocks. Hollow the chest and raise the back. Sink the shoulders and lower the elbows. Draw in the buttocks. Bend both arms with the fingers pointing forward and the palms facing downward.

Extending the Ch'i, to the side

Movement:

Keeping the hands, arms and knees in place, use the energy of your waist and legs and at your discretion perform a shaking motion one or two hundred times.

After completing these shaking motions, separate both arms levelly to the left and right sides with the fingers stretched outwards and the palms facing downwards. Again perform a shaking motion one or two hundred times.

Lastly, rotate the body (to the left side and then the right side) to circulate the blood and ch'i. This will put the body and mind in good spirits. What could be more advantageous than this? Consequently, this exercise is really indescribable!

2. CH'UANG PU OF T'AI CHI CH'UAN

The *Ch'uang Pu* [2] (Post Stances) of T'ai Chi Ch'uan are divided into two types: *Ma Pu* [3] and *Ch'uan Tzu* [4]. Previous generations who practiced the T'ai Chi Ch'uan forms first practiced the two forms of stances (Ma Pu and Ch'uan Tzu). This would make it possible for the chin (intrinsic energy) to be developed in the lower extremities (feet and legs), so as to prevent drifting and floating.

The present generation prefers to train within the confines of pushing-hands. For this reason there are these methods of stance training, which are similar to that of building a foundation for a house. The foundation must be strong; otherwise, it could not support the topmost chambers in a high tower or the high ceilings of a large mansion. How could a weak foundation support anything above it?

Unfortunately few students take this work to hand. In order to gradually progress, begin practicing the circular forms and pushing-hands; but take note, inexperience in these kung-fu stances has the consequence of there being no skill in the legs and feet and your center of balance can easily be tilted.

Earlier writings on this subject urged that these stances be learned and that great attention be paid to them. If these stances are foregone then when performing the circular forms, the legs will not be seated firmly and you will not find precision in the posture movements. Likewise, when performing pushing-hands, with one easy pull that person will be bent over; with one push his center of balance will be disrupted and he will be thrown back. Consequently, if you wish to train in true kung-fu and do not practice Ch'uang Pu, you will be unsuccessful; these must be practiced! It is unimportant whether the period of practice is long or short, the important thing is to establish consistency. Simply do them on a regular basis. Even after one month they will prove their effectiveness. The following is a breakdown of the training procedures.

STANDING POST HORSE STANCE[5]

Maintain the center of balance (weight) between the two legs, with the upper torso upright and straight. Suspend the head and relax the waist. Hollow the chest and raise the back. Sink the shoulders and hang the elbows downward. The wei lu (coccyx region) is centered and upright. The eyes gaze intently at the hands. Gather the ch'i and concentrate the spirit. Inhale and exhale through the nose. Bend and curve the two arms, with

Standing Post Horse Stance

both hands out front and the palms directly facing one another as if holding a ball.

Now distinguish between doing an ascent and descent with the body. The *ascent:* the body rises slightly upwards and the two hands open slightly. Work the ch'i on the inhalation and adhere it to the spine. On the *descent* the body moves slightly downward into a seated position and the hands close slightly. Work the ch'i on the exhalation and sink it into the tan-tien.

Brief summary: The two hands open and close once during each complete breath. They operate on a similar basis to the motion of the lungs when one is breathing.

Beginners should pause five minutes in this position (after rising and sinking numerous times). Gradually pause for a longer and longer period of time (possibly thirty minutes or so).

Afterwards, through time, the lower extremities (waist, legs and feet) will acquire the skill of rootedness and the four limbs and entire body will have intrinsic energy. Externally everything will be substantially augmented and internally the tan-tien will be well nourished.

3. STANDING POST CH'UAN TZU STYLES

Stand erect. Step out with the right foot one half a step to the front and place the heel on the ground with the toes raised slightly upwards. Bend the left leg. Separate the two feet so they are about one foot apart. The upper body is upright and the buttocks do not protrude. Hollow the chest and raise the back. Retain a light and nimble energy on top of the head. Center the wei lu so that it is upright. Do not wander in thought or be anxious.

Ch'uan Tzu, right

With each inhalation adhere the ch'i to the spine. With each exhalation sink the ch'i into the tan-tien.

Move the body down into a low squatting position, with the greater part of the body's weight on the left leg. Bend the two arms slightly and extend both hands forward. Sink the shoulders and hang the elbows. Straighten the wrists; bend the fingers slightly. They should be divided and open (relaxed). The right hand is in front and the left hand is behind, being somewhat close to the front of the chest. The palms face one another, but are not parallel.

The upper body consists of shoulders, elbows and wrists. The lower body consists of hips, knees and feet. Each of them are related - shoulders and hips, elbows and knees, wrists and feet.

The entire body should be light and nimble, without a trace of external muscular exertion. It is essential to seek naturalness.

Ch'uan Tzu, left

This style is contained within the *Thirteen Postures* [7], *Lifting Hands*, and is exactly the same as Ch'uan Tzu. This acts as the right style.

The left style of Ch'uan Tzu is similar to the right style; the difference being that the left hand and left foot are extended out to the front. The appearance of the left style is just like that of the posture, *Hands Playing The Guitar*, which is contained within the Thirteen Postures of the ch'uan form.

When practicing the forms of post stances, no matter whether for long or short periods, be consistent in your practice. Both the mind-intent and ch'i are internal. Within one's body, especially the waist and legs, is the kung-fu of intrinsic energy. Each of these: mind-intent, ch'i and intrinsic energy have limitless benefit.

Below are examples of the Eight Postures of Ch'uang Pu (Post Stances)

Ward-Off

Roll-Back

Press

Push

Repulse Monkey (Pull)

Diagonal Flying (Split)

Strike Tiger (Elbow-Stroke)

Shoulder-Stroke

Within the posture Push there is *advancing, withdrawing, looking-left, gazing-right* and *central equilibrium.* They are contained within the post stances, and the weapon styles. These, "*Five Attitudes,*" are very important within any of the T'ai Chi Ch'uan practices.

Previous generations trained in these kung-fu stances ten years or more, every day without fail. They did this to develop these postures and attain the results of the cultivation of mind-intent , spirit and ch'i. Therefore, if taking up the practice of T'ai Chi Ch'uan, do so without negligence. In regards to all the other solo postures (The Thirteen Postures of T'ai Chi Ch'uan) any one of them will do for practicing post stances. Ideally practice each one as a post stance.

This type of solo posture practice was performed from ancient times up to Yang Chien-hou[9] in the final years of the Ch'ing Dynasty[10]. It was handed down from teacher to pupil. Its importance should be quite evident.

4. TSAI-TUI METHOD[11]

Within this boxing art are the tsai-tui method and the much more vicious *ch'ih tui* [12] method. Flying Leg uses the toes and a high climbing kick to your opponent. Tsai-tui employs the sole of the foot to strike the opponent's knee cap or to go directly into the bone. It is used in a similar manner to picking up the foot to walk. The power of this method is great and all who experience its ferocity suffer serious injury.

There are many uses of this kicking technique within T'ai Chi Ch'uan, yet few understand the meaning. They are fearful of injury when dealing with an opponent and seek only kicks which are thought safe and solid. Without training in the tsai-tui method they cannot acquire even this.

The training method is to use the right foot as if employing tsai to an opponent. The right hand does the work of leading and grasping towards the rear (pulling his arm to the back and downward diagonally). The left palm is directed forward, like lightning to the opponent's face. The hand and arm are kept in a bent position. Simultaneously the sole of the right foot is moved as if being pulled forward and down. When pulling, the body is turned slightly sideways as it is moved down into a squatting position. Both hands are simultaneously opened to the front and back. The left knee is slightly bent and the weight is entirely on the left leg.

In the upper body, the chest is hollowed and the back raised. The ch'i is sunk into the tan-tien. A light and sensitive energy is retained on top of the head. The waist is seated and the pelvis is relaxed.

When it is the left foot which performs tsai-tui, the left hand does the work of leading and grasping towards the rear. The right palm is extended to the opponent's face like lightning. The left foot is simultaneously moved forward and down to perform

Tsai-Tui

tsai. The right knee is bent slightly and the weight is placed entirely upon it. The remainder is like that in the previous style.

These types, the left and right styles of tsai-tui, should be practiced simultaneously. After a long period of training the entire body will undergo a change and the four limbs will be able to move as one unit externally. Also, the waist and legs will acquire *tso ching*. Otherwise, when wanting to kick with the leg to an opponent, one foot will not rise properly because the other foot will be floating. Thus, the opponent will not be knocked down, but you, yourself will have fallen over.

Train in these solo styles of tsai-tui, for if you learn them you will not be caught unawares.

Original Illustrations

Extending the Ch'i

*Standing Post Horse Stance
(Ma Pu Chan Ch'uang)*

Chuan Tzu (left)

Chuan Tzu (right)

Ward-Off   Roll-Back

Press   Push

Repulse Monkey   Diagonal Flying

Strike Tiger   *Shoulder-Stroke*

Tsai-Tui

CHAPTER SIX NOTES

1.The idea here is to internally create a vibration, originating in the tan-tien and coming through the spine, through the shoulders and spine and then out the fingers. But this vibration is not to be violent or forced. This practice is similar to that of t'ai chi sword, wherein the blade of the sword is caused to vibrate by using the whole body as one unit.

In this exercise make use of the heng ha sounds with a short inhalation and long exhalation, but do so inaudibly.

The purpose of this exercise is twofold: 1) In the T'ai Chi Ch'i-Kung exercise you are stimulating and accumulating ch'i. This exercise then harmonizes the body by releasing it so that "scorching ch'i" is not developed. 2) A foundation for learning to issue ch'i off the spine and out the finger tips. Later when you develop chin (intrinsic energy) this will enhance your ability for *fa chin* (issuing energy).

2. CH'UANG PU: *Post Stance.* Ch'uang has two primary meanings: 1) A post or stake, and 2) A buoy. The idea being expressed is that of root and centeredness.

3. MA PU: *Horse Stance*, like riding a horse.

4. CH'UAN TZU: *Ch'uan Tzu* is an untranslatable compound. The character here, Ch'uan (川), is descriptive of how the body appears in this stance.

5. MA PU CHAN CH'UANG: *Standing Post Horse Stance.*

6. CH'UAN TZU SHIH CHAN CH'UANG: *Standing Post Ch'uan Tzu Styles.* The Ch'uan Tzu Styles are both the *Lifting Hands* posture (Ti Shou) and *Hands Playing the Guitar* (Shou Hui Pi Pa) of T'ai Chi Ch'uan.

7. SHIH SAN SHIH: *Thirteen Postures.* Normally shih is translated as "postures," but should be considered more as power, strength and influential activity. These thirteen postures are the primary functions of T'ai Chi Ch'uan.

In earlier T'ai Chi Ch'uan history, the form was originally called Thirteen Posture T'ai Chi Ch'uan. The names of the postures are:
1) *Ward-Off*
2) *Roll-Back*
3) *Press*
4) *Push*
5) *Pull*
6) *Split*
7) *Elbow-Stroke*
8) *Shoulder-Stroke*
(The above eight are normally associated with The Eight Diagrams. See Note 12, Chapter One.)
9) *Advance*
10) *Withdraw*
11) *Look-Left*
12) *Gaze-Right*
13) *Central Equilibrium*
(The above five represent *The Five Activities*)

In brief, the eight postures are the basis for all T'ai Chi Ch'uan postures. The Five Activities are aspects of each posture. Hence, there are not really thirteen postures. It would probably be better to translate this as "thirteen principle functions".

8. **WU HSING:** *The Five Activities.* (See Note 12, Chapter One). The Five Activities are Metal (Advance), Wood (Withdraw), Water (Look-Left), Fire (Gaze-Right) and Earth (Central Equilibrium). Each posture of T'ai Chi Ch'uan contain these five activities.

9. **YANG CHIEN-HOU:** (1842-1917) Second son of Master Yang Lu-Chan (1799-1872), the founder of Yang Style T'ai Chi Ch'uan.

10. **CH'ING CHI:** Ch'ing Dynasty 1644 to 1908.

11. **TSAI-TUI:** *Plucking and Kicking* or *Pulling With Kick.* The meaning of tsai is to pluck, like a flower, in which one hand holds the base of the stem and the other plucks the flower. This exercise is the basis for the T'ai Chi Ch'uan postures employing a kick. This method is a combination of extending the ch'i (Part One, this chapter) and ch'uang pu (Part Two, this chapter).

12. **CH'IH TUI:** *Flying Leg.* This is a method developed by the Shaolin Ch'uan sect. The kick in this method is directed to the opponent's head, whereas in tsai-tui it is directed at the opponent's knee.

About the Translator

Stuart Alve Olson began learning the Chinese language during his residency at the City of Ten-Thousand Buddhas in Ukiah, CA (1979-1980). In 1982 he was invited to live in Master Liang's home in St. Cloud, Minnesota (the only student granted this honor). Staying with Master Liang for five years, Stuart studied both T'ai Chi Ch'uan and Chinese language under his tutelage. Since that time he has travelled extensively throughout the United States with Master Liang assisting him in teaching T'ai Chi Ch'uan. Stuart has also taught in Canada, Indonesia and travelled throughout Asia. He lives in Minneapolis, Minnesota where he both teaches T'ai Chi Ch'uan and compiles and translates various Chinese philosophical, martial arts and health oriented books for Dragon Door Publications.

A

accomplishment, 58
advancing and withdrawing, 40
advancing attitude, 150, 158
after heaven breath, 29, 47, 55, 64
attitudes, five, 150, 158

B

before heaven breath, 29, 47, 55, 65
blood, 37-38
body and ch'i, 37
Book of Mencius, The, 70
breath, lower level, 47, 50, 55
breath, natural, 12-13, 33-34
breath, one, 38, 44-45
breath, reverse, 12, 33-34
breath, short, 49
breath, upper level, 47, 50, 55
breathing with movement, 48
breathing, deep, 76-77
bright ch'i, 20
brute-force, 28

C

central equilibrium attitude, 150, 158
ch'eng chiang, 65, 72
ch'i, 19, 27, 37-42, 43, 47-54, 75
ch'i hai, 67, 72
ch'i, bright, 20. *See also* positive ch'i.
ch'i, circulating the, 47
ch'i, extending the, 139-141
ch'i, mobilizing the, 47-54
ch'i, negative, 12, 41-42

ch'i, positive, 41-42
ch'i, scorching, 157. *See also* negative ch'i.
ch'i-kung, 12
ch'iao chin, 33
ch'ien, 72
ch'ih tui method, 150, 159
Ch'ing Chi, 158
Ch'ing Dynasty, 158
ch'uan, 39
ch'uan tzu, 21, 141, 143-150, 157
ch'uang pu, 141-150, 157
ch'uang pu, eight postures of, 146-149
Chang San-feng, 16, 138
Chen Tuan, 138
Chen Yen-lin, 15-17
Chen, Yearning K., 16–17
chin, 45
chin tan, 70
ching, 14, 37, 43–44, 70–71
ching li, 34
ching shen, 32
ching, conservation of, 44
cho-li, 33
Chung Li-ch'uan, 138
chung lou, 66, 69, 72
chung tan-tien, 72
circuit, 138
circulating the ch'i, 47
Complete Reality Sect, 138
concentration, fixed, 69
Confucianism, 70
cross-legged posture, 59, 60

D

death, peaceful, 31
deep breathing, 76–77

diagonal flying posture, 148
directly arrive at heaven's
    heart, 67
dispersing-hands, 45
divine water, 72
double fish symbol, 62
dragon, green, 50

E

earth bound spirit, 45
earthly immortal, 45
Eight Immortals, 138
eight pieces of brocade, 138
eight postures of ch'uang pu,
    21, 146–149
eighteenth gesture, 126–127
eighth gesture, 94–95
elbow-stroke posture, 149
eleventh gesture, 100–103
elixir, field of, 44
elixir, golden, 57, 70
elixir, internal, 37
embrace the sun and moon,
    67
energies, 27, 33
energies, intrinsic, 28, 33, 45,
    70
energy, issuing, 157
energy, seating, 159
exercises, training, 139–152
extending the ch'i exercise,
    21, 138–141

F

fa chin, 157
fei, 61
field of elixir, 44
fifteenth gesture, 120–121
fifth gesture, 88–89
fire and water, 44

first gesture, 78–79
five activities. See five
    attitudes.
five attitudes, 150, 158
five element theory, 34
five thieves, 71
five viscera, 71
flying leg method, 150, 159
fourteenth gesture, 118–119
fourth gesture, 86–87
fu hsi diagram, 29, 62
full lotus posture, 59
fullness and emptiness, 40

G

gate of life, 37, 43
gazing-right attitude, 150,
    158
gestures, 78–133
golden bell kung, 56
golden elixir, 57, 70
graphics, an explanation of,
    18–19
great accomplishment, 58
great roll-back, 45
greater heavenly circuit,
    67–69
green dragon, 50
guard the one, 31

H

h'un, 45
ha, 53, 55
hai ti, 51, 55
half lotus posture, 59, 60
Han Chung-li, 138
hands playing the guitar, 145,
    157
hands, dispersing. See
    dispersing-hands.

hands, pushing. *See* pushing-hands.

heat, scorching, 20

heaven's heart, directly arrive at, 67

heaven, after, 29, 45

heaven, before, 29, 47

heavenly circuits, 66–69

heavenly immortal, 45

heng, 53, 55

heng ha, 52–54, 55–56

horse stance, 139, 142–143

hou t'ien, 29, 33–34, 47, 55

hsaio chou t'ien, 72

hsia tan-tien, 72

hsia ts'eng chi, 55

hsien t'ien, 29, 33–34, 47, 55

hsin, 60

hsuan kuan, 66, 72

hundred illnesses, 31

huo shui, 44

I

I, 61. *See also* mind-intent.

i k'ou ch'i, 44–45

i-ch'i, 45

I-Ching, 72

illnesses, hundred, 31

illustrations, original, 134–137, 153–156

imagination, follow the, 40

immortals, three stages of, 45

in the field, 67

inhaling and exhaling, 40

internal art, T'ai Chi Ch'uan as, 11

internal boxing art, 39

internal breathing methods, 47–54

internal elixir, 37

intrinsic energies, 28, 33, 45, 70

issuing energy, 157

J

Jade Emperor's Mind-Seal Classic, 44

K

k'un, 72

kan, 60

king wen diagram, 30

kuan yuan, 67, 73

kung, 30–31, 34, 69, 73

kung-fu, 69, 73

Kung-fu Tzu, 58, 70

L

Lao Tzu, 44

letting down the screens, 59

li, 33

lifting hands posture, 145, 157

ling t'ai, 66, 72

looking-left attitude, 150, 158

lower level breath, 47, 50, 55

lower tan-tien, 20

Lu Tung-pin, 138

M

ma pu, 141, 157. *See also* horse stance.

Master Liang, 15, 22–23

meditation, 57–61

meditation, seated, 43

Mencius. *See* Meng Tzu.

Meng Tzu, 58, 70

Mental Elucidation of the Thirteen Kinetic Postures, 35, 40, 41, 48

middle tan-tien, 20
mind-intent, 19–20, 37,
    39–42, 43
ming-men, 43
Mt. Kunlun, 67

N

natural breath, 12, 33–34
negative ch'i, 12, 41–42
ni-wan, 55
nineteenth gesture, 128–129
ninth gesture, 96–97
nourishing-life, 19, 32

O

one breath, 38, 44–45
opening and closing, 40
Origin, the, 31
original illustrations,
    134–137, 153–156
Original Yang Style of T'ai
    Chi Ch'uan, The, 14, 159

P

p'i, 61
p'o, 38, 45–46, 61
pa tuan chin, 76–77
pa tuan chin, 138
Pao Yuan, 34
peaceful death, 31
plant the jade, rest and
    plough, 69
positive ch'i, 41–42
post stances, 141–150, 157
postures, four initial, 45
postures, four primary, 45
practice, 11, 29
press posture, 147
pure immortal, 45
push posture, 147
pushing-hands, 28, 45

R

repulse monkey posture, 148
returning to spring, 69
reverse breath, 12, 34
ride the black ox through the
    dark valley pass, 67
roll-back posture, 45, 146
roll-back, great, 45

S

saliva, 72
san-shou, 45
San-Shou, Tui-Shou and Ta-
    Lu of T'ai Chi Ch'uan, 14
scorching ch'i, 157. *See also*
    negative ch'i.
scorching heat, 20
seating energy, 159
second gesture, 80–81
seeing a dragon at the bottom
    of the sea, 67
seventeenth gesture, 124–125
seventh gesture, 92–93
sexual fluids, 43
shan chung, 66, 69, 72
shan ken, 65, 72
shang tan-tien, 72
shang ts'eng chi, 55
Shaolin Ch'uan, 27
shen, 28, 44
sheng, 60
shih san shih, 157
short breath, 49
shou-i, 34
shoulder-stroke posture, 149
sitting practice, 59–63
sixteenth gesture, 122–123
sixth gesture, 90–91
skillful energy, 33

small accomplishment, 58
small heavenly circuits, 20, 66
small rest at the Central Mt.
  Hsu Mi, 67
Song of Thirteen Postures,
  The, 42
sperm, 43
spirit, 28
spirit, earth bound. See earth
  bound spirit.
 spirit, sentient. See earth
  bound spirit.
split posture, 148
stamina, 29, 34
standing post ch'uan tzu
  styles, 143–150
standing post horse stance,
  21, 142–143, 157
stillness, 57–59, 70
strength, 33
strike tiger posture, 149
sung, 21, 44

T
T'ai Chi Ch'i-Kung, 12, 67,
  75–138
T'ai Chi Ch'uan Classic of
  Secret Songs, 53
T'ai Chi Ch'uan for Health
  and Self-Defense, 15
T'ai Chi Ch'uan Treatise, 54
T'ai Chi Ch'uan: Its Effects
  and Practical Applications,
  17
T'ai Chi Sword, Sabre and
  Staff, 13, 14, 159
t'ien hsien, 45
t'ien hsin, 72
t'ien ling point, 51, 55

ta-lu, 38, 45
tan-tien, 19–20, 37, 39, 44,
  67
tan-tien, abiding by the, 19,
  20, 44
Tao Te Ching, 44
Tao yin, 138
teacher, importance of having
  a, 49
techniques without principles,
  39
ten-thousand images, 69
tenth gesture, 98–99
thieves, five, 71
third gesture, 82–85
thirteen postures, 145,
  157–158
thirteenth gesture, 112–117
Three Treasures, The, 19
ti hsien, 45
tiger, white, 50
training exercises, 139–152
Treasures, The Three, 19
tsai-tui method, 21, 150–152,
  158–159
tu fu, 66, 72
tuan lien, 32
tui-shou, 28, 38, 45
Tui-Shou, San-Shou, and Ta-
  Lu of Yang Style T'ai Chi
  Ch'uan, 159
twelfth gesture, 104–111
twentieth gesture, 130–131
twenty-first gesture, 132–133

U
upper level breath, 47, 50, 55
upper tan-tien, 20

V

vibration, 157
viscera, five, 71
vitality, 27

W

ward off posture, 146
water, divine, 72
wei lu, 51, 55
white tiger, 50
will. See mind-intent.
withdrawing attitude, 150,
    158
Wo Ho-ching, 16
wu hsing, 158
wu-chi, 61, 67
wu-tsang, 71
wu-tse, 71

Y

Yang Cheng-fu, 15–16
Yang Chien-hou, 150, 158
Yang family, 15–16
yang fire, 50
yang hsien, 45
Yang Lu-chan, 16, 158
yang, advancing the, 50
Yang-Sheng, 19, 32
yen hsien, 72
yin convergence, 50
yin, withdrawing the, 50
Yin-Yang theory, 34
yu chen point, 51, 55
yu chu, 66, 72
yuan shen, 45
yung chuan, 67

The Jade Emperor's Mind Seal Classic
A Taoist Guide to Health,
Longevity and Immortality

Translated by Stuart Alve Olson,
$10.95, paper, 128 pages,
15 illustrations
ISBN 0-938045-10-5

The Taoists believes that there is no reason for a person to ever suffer physical illness. Death itself, whether from old age or sickness, is an unnecessary occurence. Illness and death occur as a result of the dissipation of the Three Treasures - *ching, ch'i and shen* - our reproductive, life-sustaining and spiritual energies. The secret science of restoring, gathering and transforming these primal energies creates an elixir which will confer health, longevity and immortality.

The Jade Emperor's Mind Seal Classic, presented here in the first English translation, is a primer on how to achieve these benefits. A supreme distillation of Taoist thought, the text works as the catalyst for a deep transformation of the being.

Stuart Olson, Taoist practitioner and long-time protege of Taoist and T'ai Chi Ch'uan master, T.T. Liang, provides a lucid translation of, and an insightful commentary on this key text. With its wealth of practical information the commentary will further reward the reader with deeper insights into other great Taoist works, such as *The Secret of the Golden Flower* and *Taoist Yoga: Alchemy and Immortality.*

Olson supplements this classic with a further translation of a rare treatise on *The Three Treasures of Immortality* taken from the Dragon Door sect of Taoism. A collection of aphorisms and quotes from various Taoist scriptures and masters, *The Three Treasures of Immortality,* sheds further light on the processes that will lead you to enhanced health and longevity, if not enlightenment and immortality.

Imagination Becomes Reality
The Teachings of
Master T.T. Liang

Compiled by Stuart Alve Olson
$19.95, paper, 292 pages,
7" x 11", 600 illustrations.
ISBN O-938045-09-1

T.T. Liang is one of the most revered living masters of T'ai Chi Ch'uan. Now in his nineties, he has taught T'ai Chi for over fifty years. As a senior student to Cheng Man-ch'ing and as author of the best-selling T'ai Chi Ch'uan for Health and Self-Defense he helped introduce T'ai Chi to America.

This book presents the very heart of Liang's teachings, including his own version of the Yang style 150 posture solo form. Taken from T.T.'s own notes, this is the most comprehensive description of the form ever presented. Rare interviews and articles by T.T. Liang explore the basic principles and meaning of this increasingly popular martial art.

The remarkable photography both captures the full power, grace and subtlety of T'ai Chi while providing a detailed count by count presentation of each posture.

"Master T.T. Liang is a Chinese martial arts treasure in Western society. He was a true pioneer in the development of T'ai Chi Ch'uan in the United States of America."
— Dr. Yang Jwing-ming,
author of Yang Style T'ai Chi Ch'uan

"This profound yet practical book...has much to offer practitioners of T'ai Chi and those intrigued by the concept of heightened awareness."
—Australian Bookseller and Publisher